"Like Dixon, most of us can imagine ourse_____ pity if we suddenly found ourselves paralyzed from the chest down. Dixon has authored this tightly written memoir with humor, honesty, intrigue, and unsentimental appreciation for the significant people who helped him when he was down—from therapists to smart-aleck middle school students. Most of all, this story brims with hope in an unrelentingly gracious God who won't let go."

—Rev. Mark Stephenson
Director of Disability Concerns
Christian Reformed Church in North America

"In a tale marked by ironic self-reflection, wry humor, and brutal honesty, Relentless Grace takes us along on a gripping search for meaning in the midst of tragedy. Dixon is a disarmingly clever guide, introducing us to unforgettable characters that shape the course of this compelling journey. Crisp, vivid prose unravels a subtle mystery within an emerging sense of hope and rebirth. You'll chuckle and weep as God's healing love and unfailing grace paint surprising patterns in an intimate portrait of hard-won understanding. Inspiring, gut-wrenching and beautifully rendered, Relentless Grace is both a moving personal story and a courageous illumination of God's invitation to give hope another chance."

—Jan Coates
Author/Speaker/Consultant
President and founder www.setfreetoday.com

RELENTLESS
GRACE

GOD'S INVITATION TO GIVE HOPE ANOTHER CHANCE

RELENTLESS
GRACE

A MEMOIR

RICH DIXON

WINEPRESS WP PUBLISHING

WinePress Publishing (PO Box 428, Enumclaw, WA 98022) functions only as book publisher. As such, the ultimate design, content, editorial accuracy, and views expressed or implied in this work are those of the author.

Unless otherwise noted, all Scriptures are taken from the *Holy Bible, New International Version*®, *NIV*®. Copyright © 1973, 1978, 1984 by the International Bible Society. Used by permission of Zondervan. All rights reserved.

ISBN 13: 978-1-57921-958-1
ISBN 10: 1-57921-958-6
Library of Congress Catalog Card Number: 2008923131

To Al
You showed me where to search

To Pete
You showed me how to search

To Becky
You gave me a reason to search

CONTENTS

Acknowledgments xi

Introduction xiii

Prologue xvii

1. Two Faces 1

2. The Mountains 9

3. Church 15

4. Running 23

5. The Steps 31

6. The Monster in the Mirror 37

7. Heaven 51

8. Happy Valentine's Day 59

9. Elevator 83

10. Leonard 99

11. Back to School 113

12. Three Wise Guys 119

13. Pete 129

14. Center 141

15. That Pesky Question 157

Epilogue 161

ACKNOWLEDGMENTS

I've learned many important lessons in the process of writing my first book. Books don't just magically materialize, and they're never the work of a single person. So even though I get to list myself as the author, the efforts of several talented professionals contributed to the final product.

Liz McGrew edited the first, very rough, draft. Michael Garrett provided extremely valuable content and organizational assistance as well as professional formatting. Mary McNeil polished the final draft and provided much-needed encouragement. Any errors that remain, despite the best advice of these three wonderful editors, are the responsibility of a rookie author.

I am grateful to Elizabeth Geiser and Jan Coates for guiding a novice through the murky waters of the publishing world. This book would not exist without their patient answers to a thousand questions, large and small.

I've also learned the rare nature of truly original ideas and the concrete meaning of this old phrase: *Stealing from one source is called plagiarism, while stealing from multiple sources is called research.* You don't realize how much your thoughts are the product of others' work until you begin writing them. Advance apologies to those who may find their own words mirrored a bit too closely.

Finally, there are no phrases to sufficiently express my gratitude to the characters of the story. Each of them contributed in a special and significant manner to my eventual recovery from a serious injury. I am here because of their patience and kindness in bleak circumstances. The amazing story of this book is the result of their unfailing kindness, generosity and friendship.

INTRODUCTION

Whenever someone says, "God told me to do this," I'm afraid I tend to respond with some mixture of skepticism and jealousy.

I'm skeptical because I suspect "this is what God wants" often justifies what we were going to do anyway. "God's will" becomes a convenient excuse to rationalize a broad range of choices that frequently conform more to our personal wishes than to God's direction.

I'm jealous because I am often unable to distinguish God's voice from the clamor of circumstances and the confusion of my own thoughts. I wish for the wisdom to discern "what God wants" within the chaos of conflicting values and competing interests. I believe God prepares a path for each of us, but I confess that I frequently fail to clearly perceive His direction.

That said, I'm convinced God directed me during the last fifteen years on a carefully calculated journey. I believe He methodically and persistently guided me through a series of experiences that prepared me to tell the tale of *Relentless Grace* and to invite you to hear His message of hope through the events of the story. In retrospect, opportunities and challenges that made no sense in isolation assume unmistakable significance in the context of His patient leadership.

The account is not easy to relate because its episodes expose profound personal weakness. A confluence of accident and horrible decisions conceived a nightmare that threatened to permanently envelope me in a cloud of darkness and hopelessness.

Many times during the voyage people said, "You ought to write a book," but I knew I lacked sufficient insight to detect pattern or form in apparently pointless experiences. While I was flattered that my friends thought I could actually write a book, I didn't seriously consider that coherent significance might be concealed within a seemingly jumbled tangle of occurrences. I could not imagine how others might benefit from reading my messed-up personal story.

Then about four years ago I encountered "You ought to write a book" once again, and for no discernable reason I noticed an unfamiliar sense of clarity. A twisted web of misfortune and mistake assumed focus and organization. I opened a new file on my computer and began tapping the keyboard as though I was repeating an old, familiar tale. The words on the screen revealed an account of God's work in the circumstances of my life, His refusal to allow me to give up, and His perfect faithfulness in the face of my incessant lack of faith.

I discovered a cogent message concealed within the seemingly random episodes of an unremarkable story of hopelessness. I'd been focused on the dreadful details, but now I recognized from a broader perspective a beautiful impressionist mosaic. God used an ordinary life to reveal an extraordinary invitation: *give hope another chance.*

This book is not about an awful accident or the magical rekindling of a love dormant for too long; in fact, it's not really about me at all. The story only provides context for the true substance of the narrative.

This book is about hope. It's about God, about forgiveness, about promises made and kept even in the midst of grief and loss. It's about knowing with absolute certainty that Jesus walks with us, that He knows our pain and fear and will help us not simply to survive but to thrive in the most difficult and overwhelming situations.

This book is about the God who refused to allow me to throw away the life He created, who looked past my disobedience and harmful choices and demonstrated His unfailing love by using a potentially life-destroying calamity to reveal possibilities I could never have imagined. It's about love so deep and wide that even His Son was not too great a price to pay for its fulfillment. It's about love I've done nothing to deserve, freely given by grace.

INTRODUCTION

I perceived only an incomprehensible, meaningless clutter and an existence devoid of hope, but God offered an alternative view. Where I saw a tangle of loose threads, God showed me His perspective. Apparently hopeless chaos was really the reverse side of a beautiful tapestry woven patiently by the God who works for good in all circumstances. He gathered the shattered remnants of a life broken by evil and created for me a priceless work of art, not because of anything I did but simply because He loves me.

This book is about Jesus' selfless sacrifice that invites you and me to experience healing and hope. It's about mercy that allows me to escape the rightful consequences of my actions and decisions. It's about grace that offers undeserved hope and abundance, freely given despite repeated attempts at rejection.

I truly pray that you'll discover renewed hope along this journey guided by God's *Relentless Grace*.

Fort Collins, Colorado
February 2008

PROLOGUE

. . . let us run with perseverance the race marked out for us.
                                             —Hebrews 12:1(b)

Life's not a sprint; it's a marathon."
This common metaphor contains a good deal of truth about effective approaches to life. Sprinters tire quickly as a short burst of maximum effort depletes energy reserves. A marathoner understands the importance of pacing, replenishing fuel supplies, and conserving enough energy to complete the race. Sprinters win or lose within a few seconds, but that's not how life usually works. A longer competition requires discipline and strategy to cope with the inevitable variations in terrain, wind, and weather.

Each life contains a measure of good times and bad, joy and sadness. A balanced approach to the varying seasons of our time on Earth requires a long-term perspective if we're to survive and thrive in the circumstances we encounter along the journey.

Metaphors, however, only approximate real life. Like any metaphor, "life is like a marathon" doesn't precisely describe every situation. At some point, nearly every individual encounters an obstacle that cannot be attributed to the normal course of the race.

Imagine you're running a marathon. You're monitoring the situation, carefully maintaining a reasonable pace based on ability and training. You've prepared your body and mind for the race; you know the signs that tell you to run faster or slower, when to drink or eat.

You expect the unavoidable ebbs and flows of mental and physical energy. Hills and headwinds will increase difficulty in some places; sunshine and tailwinds will provide a few easy, enjoyable stretches. You're eager to confront exhilaration and trial as fundamental elements of the competition.

You also know about "the wall," that point where you'll be tested nearly beyond your ability. You anticipate that burning muscles and aching lungs will challenge desire and discipline. You expect the urge to give up, to stop and allow the pain to subside. The lure of immediate relief will entice you to cast aside goals and dreams, surrendering the satisfaction of the finish line in return for an end to the struggle.

You know this demanding moment of temptation lurks ahead. You're prepared for the unavoidable pain. You trust that training and experience will provide the internal resources required to endure the agony at "the wall" and complete the course.

Then, without any warning, you fall into a hole.

The publicized course didn't mention this complication. You didn't train for it, couldn't see it coming, didn't prepare survival supplies or pack climbing equipment. There's no cell phone reception in the hole.

You try everything you know to escape from the hole on your own, but all of your training, experience, and discipline are useless. No specialized diet or workout regimen could have prepared you to overcome this unanticipated challenge. You simply cannot get yourself out of the hole. You're stuck, powerless.

It's hopeless.

A doctor happens to walk by the hole. You call out, "Hey, Doc! I'm stuck down here. Can you help me?" The doctor writes a prescription and tosses down some medicine. You take the medicine, and you feel better. But you're still trapped.

One of your buddies walks by.

"Hey, can you help me out? I'm stuck down here. I've tried everything I can think of, but I can't get out."

Your friend tosses you a Bible with some inspiring passages marked. You read the passages and meditate on them, and you feel better.

But you're still caught in the hole.

Then a radical thought occurs to you: *Perhaps I should ask God for help.* (Interesting that prayer is so often the *last* thing we think of when we're in trouble.) "God," you pray, "I'm trapped in this hole and I can't get out. I've tried everything, but I'm really stuck. Can You help me?"

You hear a faint rustling sound and turn around. Jesus is there! "Lord! I'm trapped in this hole. I've tried everything, but I can't find any way out. I appreciate that You've come to be with me, but now we're both stuck here."

Jesus smiles and puts His arm on your shoulder. "Yeah," He says. "But I've been here before, and I know the way out."

We all hit "walls" in our lives. A job ends unexpectedly and finances are in shambles. A relationship ends badly and we wonder if love will ever come again. These are "walls," the stuff of life, the sort of events inherent in running the race. We want to avoid the pain, but "walls" are part of the marathon and we must encounter them at different points in our lives. They hurt, frustrate, and discourage. We're tempted to stop and give up.

At times like this we solve problems, grieve, or plan to avoid similar circumstances in the future. Like the marathon runner, we train in anticipation of life's difficult seasons. With experience, we learn to trust our mental and physical preparation and discipline to get us through the troubled times so we can continue and complete the race.

Occasionally, however, we encounter a situation we cannot overcome, a problem we cannot solve, a hole in the path for which no amount of training or experience could have prepared us.

I look up at the doctor's face. Hours in the emergency room tell me that something's very wrong.

"You're paralyzed below your chest."

Try training for that one. What sort of planning, discipline, or experience might prepare you for that pronouncement?

That's not a wall. That's a hole. You can try as hard as you wish and call on everything in your past for some tool to help you climb out. Doctors can give you medicine and friends can offer support. Doesn't change things a bit. You're in a hole.

There's no way out.

That's when Jesus shows up. He doesn't offer inspirational stories or religious platitudes. He doesn't expect you to smile and pretend that it doesn't hurt or that you're not scared to death. He knows the terror. He knows you'd give *anything* if you just didn't have to be in this hole. He feels the desperation of the prayer: "Father, if there's *any* other way, please take this cup away."

Jesus doesn't lead you in a praise song or recite an educational parable or remind you to count your blessings. He doesn't reach in His bag and pull out an inspiring devotional booklet or sit at the edge of the hole and engage in an uplifting discourse about God's goodness. He knows, because He's been there; when you're in a hole, none of that helps.

Instead, He jumps down in the hole with you. He lets go of the glory of being God of the Universe and enters into your pain and despair and fear. He shares your confinement, and He knows exactly how it feels. He's been in the hole before.

And He knows one other thing.

He knows the way out.

IS THIS WHO I THINK IT IS?

I stared intently at the seven words on my computer monitor as though additional lines might flicker on the screen and some essential insight might escape if I glanced away; squinting, afraid even to blink, expecting some subliminal communication to resolve the uncertainties flashing across my mind.

Twenty years since she left.

I searched for unseen significance concealed within the seemingly simple question, but intense scrutiny failed to wring any hidden meaning from the nineteen letters of her cryptic message. Instead, I confronted twenty years worth of unsolved mysteries.

Could the question really mean that she doesn't know "Who it is?"

How do you answer such a simple question? Where do you begin this sort of improbable, twisted tale?

CHAPTER 1

TWO FACES

A background of slate-gray clouds outlined the unfamiliar face staring down at me. I felt as if I was waking from a deep slumber, recalling the rough draft of a dream, needing a splash of cold water to clear my head and sort out the border between fantasy and reality. The face hovered over me, right there yet, somehow far away and fuzzy around the edges and I didn't know who it was or why it was there. I attempted to ask, but I couldn't manage to create the words.

I thought I was lying on my back, but I wasn't certain. Cool air washed over my face; everything seemed kind of quiet and slow and distant. No real movement, but I felt a sort of floating sensation like the gentle rocking motion of waves against the side of a boat. The clouds swayed slightly, and I realized I was being carried. Where? I tried to ask—the question formed in my mind, but no words emerged. I frowned, and he saw the expression. "Just lie still, sir. You've had an accident."

I tried to raise my head and felt something pressing against my forehead. I strained harder, but my head wouldn't move. Why? He must have seen the question in my eyes. "You're strapped to a board, sir. It's just a precaution, just to be safe. Please try to lie still."

I didn't hear the end of his attempt to reassure me as everything sort of faded away . . .

The menacing wail of the siren sounded oddly distorted, too close and intense, lacking the familiar distant echo that announces an unknown crisis. Now I sensed a different sort of motion, sudden bumps, turns, and vibrations. An engine revved, tires hummed on the road. Other peculiar sounds surrounded me from undetermined origins, squeaks and rattles as tools and equipment bounced around. I was vaguely aware of muffled voices, words obscured by the siren's deafening blare.

A tangle of tubes and cords dangled beneath the white ceiling. My head still wouldn't move so my eyes darted about, seeking clues to make some sense of the jumbled noise and movement. Indecipherable labels printed and scrawled on rows of drawers and transparent cabinet doors revealed all sorts of unfamiliar bottles and jars and packages. A monitor flashed numbers in some unintelligible code beside a bag of clear liquid suspended from a hook. Questions flashed through my thoughts, but I floated in a foggy void between being asleep and awake, aware but unable to respond.

The face reappeared above me. He noticed the puzzled expression and searching eyes. "You're in an ambulance, sir. We're almost to the hospital. Just lie still."

That's why the siren's frantic pitch sounded strange—its tone assumed a unique urgency *inside* the ambulance! I tried to understand, to perceive order within the chaos that surrounded me.

A different thump, and the gray clouds loomed above once more. I felt cool air again and the face appeared one last time. "We're at the hospital, sir. You're going to be fine. They're going to take good care of you."

Good care of me? What's wrong? Why do I need a hospital? More thoughts, but still no words materialized to express my frightened questions. What happened . . .?

A ceiling tile framed a new face. "Sir, can you hear me?" I tried to nod, but my head remained still, immobilized by the strap pressing on my forehead. She asked again, "Sir, can you talk to me?"

I finally heard my voice, weak and distant. "Yes. What . . .?"

"You've had an accident. We're going to take good care of you. Try to be calm."

Be calm? A whirl of activity surrounded my motionless body. Questions and commands volleyed back and forth in hushed tones. The atmosphere bristled with urgency, but I could only gaze at the ceiling and wonder what the rush was about. Why was everyone so concerned? Why couldn't I remember what happened?

I felt hands grabbing and pulling, gently moving my arms and legs. Scissors cut the legs of my jeans. "What's happening?" I heard myself ask quietly. The new face appeared again, bordered by the ceiling tile.

"We're just doing some tests to find out how you're doing. Can you tell me how you feel?"

The fog cleared a little. I recalled that I was in a hospital, and I surmised that the bustling environment surrounding me must be the emergency room. I heard medical conversations, dialogue from a television drama—blood pressure, pulse, IV's, x-rays. The face stared down at me. "How do you feel?"

"I can't move."

She looked away, and a brief hush settled over the room. Her gaze returned to me. "That's OK," she said. "Don't worry. The paramedics strapped you down to protect you. Do you feel any pain?"

"No." No pain, but what? Something odd, what is it? I seemed to be suspended within a sort of haze. Everything appeared slow, quiet, and far away, and still I wasn't sure . . . "What happened?"

"You fell. You've had an accident. The doctor will be here soon."

More voices all around me and questions that seemed to drift from miles away. Can you feel this? Does this hurt? Can you move this? I don't think I understood or responded.

The face and the ceiling tile emerged from the fog. "Can you hear me?"

I could, but her features appeared dim and indistinct, and I couldn't quite fashion a reply. Disembodied voices surrounded me, their muffled exchanges mingled with a confusing array of beeps and alarms from medical sensors and monitors. I heard footsteps enter and leave, but I could see only the ceiling tile and that solitary face.

". . . can you hear me?" The haze cleared again, and the face peered to me once more.

"Yes," I murmured. I heard the voices more distinctly, and some of it made more sense—and now I heard a new, more commanding voice, strong and impatient, barking orders. Clearly this voice demanded action. Get this, RIGHT NOW, get your a—moving; finally some familiar language. I smiled weakly at the ceiling tile. "Who . . .?"

The face again, "That's the doctor, Dr. Warson. He's going to take good care of you."

The world assumed some sort of order. I remembered. Ambulance. Paramedic. ER. A whirl of activity surrounded me, some kind of accident. But what's wrong? "What kind of doctor?"

That gentle face looked away, the other voices quieted as her eyes returned to me. "A neurosurgeon, one of the best. He's going to take good care of you."

For the first time, I began to understand. A neurosurgeon. They kept asking me if I felt pressure, touch, or pain, and if I could move my fingers and toes. And I couldn't. "Am I paralyzed?"

The face looked away again, toward the unseen others. "We don't know what's wrong yet. Try to relax and let us check you out. You'll be fine. We'll take good care of you."

I started to know, to comprehend the first flickers of fear. The gentle face assured me it was all right. But it wasn't all right. I couldn't feel, couldn't move, and now I began to appreciate the seriousness of my circumstances. The concern in the voices and the rush to accomplish a hundred tasks at once finally penetrated the fog. As I stared up at the ceiling tile, an incomprehensible icy terror clutched at my soul.

Paralyzed!

That only happens in the tragedy of a morbid nightmare; movie characters and football players get paralyzed. But the sounds and smells of this real-life trauma center were not props from some artificial, antiseptic movie set; no cameras recorded this horrific scene;

no teammates gathered around my lifeless body. I wasn't trapped in a sleepy fantasy.

Paralyzed? How could this be happening? I can't be paralyzed!

This day began just like any other lazy Saturday. I anticipated a slow, relaxing day off, starting with the paper and that cup of coffee that's especially good when there's no rush to get out the door. Morning frost melted into a wonderful, early December Colorado day, cloudy and brisk, but not especially cold. I was scheduled to referee a high school basketball game later in the evening, but the day was mine to enjoy.

About mid-morning, I started to think about a project, something amusing and not too strenuous. I considered several options and eventually settled on a bit of outdoor Christmas decorating. Days like this were rare in December, and this one was perfect for putting some holiday lights on the house.

I gathered supplies and made a trip to the store for some missing essentials. I savored the refreshing sense of freedom as I climbed the ladder in the crisp afternoon air, recalling the pleasure of time spent on roofs doing various construction jobs. I always enjoyed the feeling of standing on a roof, surveying my domain from the top of the world. The peaceful view seemed to offer a little different perspective. Something about simply "being above it all" imparted a calming character to even difficult, backbreaking work. I'd chosen the perfect activity, a restful and relaxing way to spend this quiet early winter day.

The kid across the street heard the hammer tapping, looked up, and shouted something. I couldn't hear his words, but I smiled and waved back. The string of colored lights stretched nearly to the peak of the roof, just a few more fasteners would complete this simple task. Some hot chocolate and a football game in front of a warm fire sounded like a perfect conclusion to this lazy afternoon. Darkness would soon unveil the holiday cheer of the completed decorations.

I stood to stretch my back and inspect my kingdom one last time. I gazed across a sea of rooftops, looked down and noticed my dog sniffing along the fence in the back yard, and then—suddenly the unfamiliar face stared down at me from the clouds. I didn't remember falling, couldn't figure out where I was or what was happening.

And now I lay motionless in the emergency room, scared to death, no idea how or why I fell. What happened? I asked the question over and over and never received an answer. I simply don't remember.

I faded in and out of hazy awareness frequently during the next hours. I recall little of that time, the lack of detailed memory a true gift from God. I faintly recollect x-rays, CT scans, and a horrible claustrophobic experience in a primitive MRI scanner. The entire sequence of events felt slow and distant, like some dreadful dream from which I couldn't force myself to awaken.

I recall one fearsome detail with high-definition digital sound clarity. As that face peered down at me from the ceiling tile, I managed to plead weakly, "If I'm paralyzed, don't let me live. I want to die.

"I want to die. Please let me die."

Two faces—one a paramedic contrasted against the gray sky, the other an emergency room nurse framed by a ceiling tile. They cared for me in those first terrible moments, my escorts into a new world of pain, fear, struggle, and loss I couldn't even begin to comprehend.

I never saw either of them again, never had the opportunity to thank them for being with me at the frightful advent of a new journey. I wonder if they know anything about the path I traveled from that horrible beginning. I don't remember what they looked like, whether they were young or old, black or white. I wouldn't recognize either of them if we passed in the hospital hallways.

The paramedic helped me resume breathing, strapped me to a board, saw those first questioning looks, and comforted me as we rode together in the ambulance. I wonder if he realized the true extent of my injuries or anticipated the horrors that loomed as he handed me off to the ER nurse.

She became my connection to the commotion that swirled around me in those first terrible hours. She consoled me as I began to appreciate the awful truth. She tried to reassure me and listened to my initial reaction as I confronted the chilling reality of paralysis.

Most people, even seasoned trauma nurses, don't show up for work on an otherwise unremarkable Saturday anticipating the sort of confusion and terror she witnessed. I wonder if she recalls ushering me through the frightful evolution from bewilderment to awareness to panic.

I wonder what flashed across her mind as I whispered my fearful plea. "I want to die.

"Please. Let me die."

IS THIS WHO I THINK IT IS?

There was no way for her to know about that terrible day, about the wheelchair that became my mode of transportation, or the hundreds of large and small modifications that comprise my radically altered reality.

How would I tell her about the unexplained fall, the faces, those horrifying hours in the ER? How could I explain that my first thought was that I wanted to die? Where do you begin to build a bridge over that kind of a twenty-year gap?

How do you just announce, "Hey, by the way. I'm paralyzed."

Not exactly a common icebreaker. That sort of revelation requires a bit of additional background.

CHAPTER 2

THE MOUNTAINS

(SIX YEARS PRIOR TO THE INJURY)

Are we there yet?"

Not the bored drone of children anxious to escape the back seat of the family minivan; not the matter-of-fact status check of a weary traveler anxious to finally reach the destination at the end of a long, boring journey. The question reflected tension mixed with unrest and almost desperate excitement.

"Are we there yet? Can you see them? Where are they?"

We peered intently into the gloomy early-morning drizzle, anxious for the first glimpse of the mountains that would signify a new beginning. A quiet night across the flats of Nebraska yielded to clouds and rain at first light. But the dreary weather couldn't dampen the anticipation as we rolled westward, leaning forward as though getting a few inches closer would make the mountains materialize from the mist.

"Look! What's that?" We rolled to a stop beside the road, sitting quietly the way you do when you've rehearsed a moment so many times that you're almost shocked when it happens differently than you imagined in all of those sleepless dreams. I suppose we anticipated a bit more fanfare. Life lacks a movie sound track; no surging crescendo of mysterious music warns of impending climax. Significant events just plop down in front of you, and only recollection reveals the perfect point to insert the drum roll and violins.

Trumpets and tympani appropriately herald a conqueror's triumphant entry, but our arrival in the Promised Land wasn't marked by musical flourishes or the appearance of majestic peaks bathed in glorious morning sunlight. Instead, we confronted a simple brown sign, a nondescript roadside declaration that we were finally entering the New World.

WELCOME TO COLORFUL COLORADO

Colorado wasn't so colorful that morning, nothing but shades of gray, mist, and fog. Still, this milestone required pictures, goofy tourist-type poses, first me, then Becky tromping through the mud and standing in the rain beside this proclamation of the beginning of our new life together. Snapshots taken, then back in the car—the Promised Land is COLD this morning.

An ordinary road sign couldn't sufficiently commemorate this life-altering moment. Israelites marked the conclusion of their forty-year exodus by ceremonially crossing the Jordan River. Our improbable dream demanded something equally substantial, a significant icon to commemorate our blind leap from the edge of security. Now the question returned.

"Where are the mountains?"

We'd officially entered the mystical land of Colorado. We drove all night, each sleeping fitfully for short stretches—but neither of us got any real rest. We didn't talk about the edgy mood during the drive, but it was there, as if you could reach out and grab the uncertain blend of excitement and hesitation. All of the fears and struggles, hopes and dreams, not really believing, but wanting it more than anything. It was so close, we could feel the reality of this implausible conception without daring to consider that it might really be happening.

Anticipation. The kind you remember when you are going to your first big-league baseball game as a kid. Tomorrow? Might as well be forever as time drags by. No sleep, up way too early for a never-ending morning. Breakfast? No thanks, I'll just get my glove and wait in the car. Yeah, I know we're not leaving for four hours. That kind of anticipation.

A quick glance at a map revealed that the eastern third of Colorado is a high, semi-arid desert. We knew the state wasn't border-to-border mountains, but "knowing" didn't much matter. We pursued a dream on that rainy morning, and dreamers don't bother with maps. A dream draws its own roads. You imagine you're there—and you're there. When you're chasing a dream down an early morning country highway, you don't want to stop for directions. It's right there, just around this corner, barely over the horizon. So we rushed onward, peering through the windshield as though we might miss the Rocky Mountains if we didn't watch carefully.

"Where are the mountains?" I guess it'll be a while. Maybe we should stop for breakfast?

Easy decision. Dreamers don't need nutrition. Grab some junk food from a gas station and get back on the road. We had to find the mountains—soon! A frantic race now, toward freedom and a new start. What if the mountains we sought so desperately were an illusion, another part of the whole impossible fantasy? What if the light of this new dawn awakened us and the dream faded until we couldn't quite distinguish sleepy imaginings from reality? Excitement mingled with fear as we chased westward after this crazy notion of escape and new life.

I might have seen the conflict that morning if I had been thinking rather than fantasizing. We acted like the mountains might move if we didn't find them *right now.* But real mountains are solid and stable, and anyone who is looking for one knows it'll be there for a long time. Dreams are like that. If you really believe in a dream, you can pursue it patiently. You know it'll be there when the time is right. When you're engaged in a frenzied, desperate chase of a vision, convinced it has to happen immediately, perhaps you're not certain, afraid if you give it half a chance it'll get away before you can get it trapped and tied down.

If you're not careful, this sort of reckless pursuit can be like chasing your shadow; the faster you scramble after it, the farther away it gets. And when you chase your shadow, you have to run away from the light. It isn't the best direction in which to seek the Promised Land.

The clouds lifted a bit, the rain stopped, and the new day became lighter. The eastern plains of Colorado have their own desolate beauty, but on that long-ago day this portion of the Promised Land represented an obstacle, something to get through. Where were the mountains? Road signs announced that we were approaching Fort Collins, and we *know* it's close to the mountains.

WHERE ARE THE MOUNTAINS?

We topped a small rise, and the Rocky Mountains emerged from the fog like the outline of a ship in one of those old black-and-white war movies. We pulled to the side of the road and scrambled into the frosty air, first giggling and celebrating, then suddenly quiet as the realization settled over us.

We made it. The mountains. Finally. We were only looking at the foothills, but to us they appeared beautiful and majestic. Now the dream could finally begin.

Countless hours of planning and scheming, painting the canvas of a vision. We'll move to the mountains, start our own life, leave behind the problems and fears, live and grow and love each other. Seemed so impossible, this dream-vision-fantasy, but here it is. At last, we've reached the mountains. Now everything will be OK.

We stood there, arms around each other at the gates of the Promised Land, face to face with the new life we came here to create, and the uncertainty we wanted to elude settled around us as subtly as the brightening daylight. Nothing big to grab your attention, no real tune in the sound track, just a nearly imperceptible background rumble felt more than heard. But the uneasiness was there, as quiet and icy as the mist. I shivered, as though by shaking my shoulders I could shudder the discord away with the morning chill.

We can get quite good at ignoring what ought to be obvious. Impossible dreams and happily-ever-after fantasies make great romantic stories. Knights on white horses snatch damsels in distress from certain calamity. Luck overshadows stupidity. Good intentions triumph over bad decisions. The good guy gets the girl in spite of his goofy antics. Somehow everything turns out as it's supposed to.

Yet real-life choices involve predictable consequences, and bad decisions usually lead to undesired results. It's awfully easy to disregard the warning signs, but the ignoring doesn't change wrong to right or alter the connection between action and outcome.

An improbable dream. We'll move away and start our new lives together. If only we can get to the mountains, all of the craziness will somehow be OK.

But as hard as I tried to shake it away, uncertainty swirled over my head like the gray morning clouds, that nagging feeling almost not there and yet as real as those hills in the brightening day. A friend of mine used to say, "You can run, but you can't hide." You can't escape by driving a few hundred miles west, even at night. The fears, uncertainties, and loss, the pain you want so desperately to leave behind, all of that stuff follows you down the road. The next morning you get out of the car in the Promised Land and the whole mess is all there waiting for you.

I knew Becky felt it, too. We stood there quietly, feigning the excitement we had imagined. No discussion of the haunting uneasiness, afraid that letting it out into the light would make it real and allow it to grow.

We both thought it would be OK. It wasn't, and we both knew it, right then as soon as we saw those miserable mountains.

IS THIS WHO I THINK IT IS?

My e-mail must have been quite a surprise. Twenty years without a word, then I pop up on her computer screen in the middle of an ordinary Monday. Did her question reflect surprise or shock? Did she feel angry? Happy? Fearful?

What unspoken meaning lurked beneath the surface of this apparently simple inquiry? Why did such a common query spawn its own series of unexpected mysteries? Was I reading too much into a straightforward question? Perhaps it wasn't even a real question.

The message that prompted her puzzling response provided little information. My message contained carefully chosen words and phrases composed in anticipation of the emotions they might trigger. Perhaps if I'd written more I'd have received a reply that incorporated fewer uncertainties and more answers.

How do you begin a conversation after twenty years of silence?

CHAPTER 3

CHURCH

W ill you please go to church with me tomorrow?"
I hesitated, uncertain how to respond to Becky's unexpected
phone request. My agenda didn't include church. I did all of that as
a kid—Sunday School, confirmation classes, youth group newspaper
drives to fund a trip to New York and Washington D.C. I didn't really
see the point. I felt no connection to a bunch of old stories, like Noah's
Ark, some guy getting swallowed by a whale, and Charlton Heston
parting the Red Sea.

On the other hand, I hadn't seen much of Becky since we arrived in
the Promised Land. Within just a few days she found her own place,
got a job, and made it clear she intended to go her own way. Apparently
the fantasy of moving away to start a new life together faded quickly in
the harsh light of reality. I missed her a lot. So if church allowed me to
spend some time with her, then church it would be.

"Yeah. Church sounds great."

As I arranged to pick her up, I pondered the disappearance of a once-
magical intimacy. I feigned excitement about her invitation. I couldn't
tell her the religion thing made no sense to me. Couldn't express how
much I missed her and how lonely I felt. Couldn't share the hurt,
confusion, or apprehension.

Why doesn't she want to be with me? What happened to the dream
of making our life together in the mountains? Why did she move all
the way out here with me, away from family and friends, only to avoid
me?

I couldn't ask the haunting questions because I knew the answers. An elaborate, fragile web of denial and make-believe disintegrated under the weight of recognition. Choices built on the shifting sands of rationalization collapsed in the winds of truth. The haze concealing the unspoken recesses of an ill-conceived escape dissipated in the light of reality and exposed the self-deceit on which the entire fantasy rested.

I still dodged the same uneasy disquiet that intruded as we stood and gazed at the mountains together for the first time. The sense of foreboding grew as we drove through that night, as we snapped pictures by that big brown sign, as we waited anxiously for gloom to give way to mountains. She felt it that day just as I did, but we didn't acknowledge the uncertainty, as though denial could kill the unwelcome intruder.

There's a difference between a dream and a goal. Dreams impart a vision of what might be. They provide a necessary point of departure, but bringing a dream to fruition usually involves hard work, planning, and figuring out how to make it come to life in the real world. Achieving a goal involves training and preparing, gathering the necessary resources, and developing a strategy. A goal is a dream with a plan.

Accomplishing a goal also means taking stock of reality and being brutally realistic about its costs. Worthwhile dreams are rarely free. You pay for your dreams to become real. Sometimes you pay with effort and hard work, sometimes with sacrifice, sometimes with an honest assessment of how you need to grow or change to create the environment in which the dream can flower.

Real world dreams-come-true don't usually just drop from the sky. Perhaps in self-help books and fairy tales it's enough to just "live your dream" and everything will happen just like you imagined, but that's not how the world typically operates. Whenever someone appears to achieve easy or instant success, closer inspection generally reveals a lot of preparation and a significant period of "paying dues." Even the most intense desire to make the dream happen can't overcome a failure to understand, and being willing to pay the price.

We wanted to run away, to put all of the nasty stuff behind us, to create a fairy-tale life. We pretended we could ignore reality, but it doesn't work that way. We didn't want to look honestly at what the fairy tale would cost, what we'd have to sacrifice to convert the dream into a plan. We talked about running away; we were afraid to talk about what we were running from. Somewhere deep inside we both knew we feared the answers to important, unspoken questions. So we drove down the road ignoring the uneasiness because we didn't believe enough in the dream to expose it to the light and confront its costs.

I couldn't give a voice to my unrest as we hurried along the road that night, and I couldn't reveal my fear as we ended our too-brief phone conversation. Even to this person I thought was my soul mate, I couldn't risk exposing the turmoil that ripped me apart.

So I tried to act excited. And I was excited about seeing Becky, talking with her, and being close to her. Church was a small price to pay for a few moments of her presence.

A lot of small talk filled the uneasy space between us, and there was a sense of relief as the room became quiet and the service began. It seemed like just yesterday we couldn't find enough time to be together, that we couldn't wait to share our thoughts, feelings, hopes, and fears. What happens between two people that so quickly and completely severs such a magical connection?

I knew the answer, though I didn't want to acknowledge the obvious truth. I knew it that day as we looked at the mountains. You can't keep chasing the shadow forever, pretending not to look over your shoulder at the light. You can't just re-write the background music of life, insert a few artificial chords where they don't belong, and ignore the uncomfortable disconnect between music and story. You can, but the plot doesn't change, fantasy doesn't become reality. The mismatched music only highlights the tortured attempt to twist episodes into a script that makes no sense to anyone.

Becky wasn't certain from the beginning about this dream of escape, and I sensed her hesitation. There's a difference between wanting to step away from a crazy swirl of events spinning out of control and being ready to start a new life with someone else. She wasn't prepared for the commitment required by this radical decision, and I knew it because I knew her so well. But I wanted it so badly that I played a tragic game of mental "make-believe," pretending that once we were alone together everything would work out.

Life doesn't happen that way. You can't just deny the truth and magically exchange wrong for right. Being real with the one you love means being authentic and truthful and transparent, especially concerning the stuff you'd rather hide. But twenty years ago we didn't do it that way, for so many reasons that made no more sense then than they do now.

So we sat there together in that small church, side by side, and miles apart. The service was comfortable, familiar. Some songs, prayers I didn't really hear to a God who didn't seem to relate to me or to the turmoil churning in my heart. Everyone else appeared so contented, men with their arms around their wives, kids squirming and drawing pictures to pass the time. I thought that's where we were destined on that long night just a few weeks ago.

At one point the congregation recited The Apostles' Creed. I was surprised that after so many years I could still repeat the familiar words memorized blindly and without meaning in childhood confirmation class. One line said Jesus "descended into hell." Becky pointed to that part and whispered, "Do you believe that?"

How should I answer? The words contained no significance to me, and I had no idea whether I actually "believed" any of this stuff, or for that matter, what it might mean to believe. But I memorized and recalled that meaningless phrase, so I nodded.

She wrinkled her brow. Disapproval. Was that the wrong answer? How was I supposed to understand empty words in lines recited blindly at age twelve because that's what some teacher assigned? How could I possibly judge the truth of such an incomprehensible assertion?

Why should I care about an irrelevant cliché? Lonely and bewildered, the fantasy of the person I loved withered before my eyes. What could these pointless platitudes possibly say to the crashing confusion that swirled in my head? My world collapsed around me, and I tried to feign happiness so she would want to be with me again. Overwhelming fear strangled me as we sat there reading meaningless proclamations while I simulated understanding and pretended that I cared.

I might have asked important questions. Why was it called The Apostles' Creed? Who were the apostles, and why did they need a creed? Why do we declare together what we believe? How might these ancient expressions calm my panic and confusion? What peace, solace and significance might I discover in these words?

The Apostles' Creed

I believe in God the Father Almighty,
Maker of heaven and earth,
And in Jesus Christ his only begotten Son,
Our Lord,
who was conceived by the Holy Spirit,
born of the virgin Mary,
suffered under Pontius Pilate,
was crucified, dead and buried.
He descended into hell.
On the third day he was raised from the dead.
He ascended into heaven,
And sits at the right hand of God the Father Almighty.
From thence he shall come
to judge the living and the dead.
I believe in the Holy Spirit,
I believe in the holy catholic church,
the communion of saints,
the forgiveness of sins,
the resurrection of the body,
and the life everlasting.
Amen.

I might have found some peace that day to replace the turmoil that ripped at my soul. But life was falling apart at the seams, and I was too busy scrambling away from the light, trying anything to stop the hurt. I was too busy wanting it to be like it used to be, or like I pretended it was.

I wasn't ready to confront the truth, to turn toward the light. The questions I needed to ask and the answers that ultimately saved my life would have to wait.

The minister began to speak, a sermon about a bunch of religious nonsense. I didn't hear him anyway; I focused on Becky. She sat so close, but a chasm of unrest separated us. Why? How could I change her mind? How could I chase away the disquiet wedged between us?

The minister seemed like a nice guy. He reminded me of an old friend, a man with a gentle spirit and a good heart. I found comfort in his familiar early gray hair and calm, reassuring voice. I didn't know what the words meant, but his manner conveyed a sense of power and assurance.

The service ended. People came to greet us, welcoming the new couple. From their greetings I could tell that they assumed we were married. I knew that presumption would make Becky uncomfortable. "Where're you from? What do you do? Any kids?" They meant to put the visitors at ease, but every question stabbed at the distance between us. We escaped as quickly as possible.

"Thanks for coming with me." She felt as awkward as I did; church hadn't bridged the gap. Her invitation would not be repeated.

"Thanks for inviting me. It was nice." Here it is again. Nothing to say, couldn't express the disquiet that divided us. "How about lunch?" Please. Spend some time with me. Let me show you we can be close again.

"No, thanks. I need to get going."

CHURCH

What should I do? Cry? Yell? Beg? Demand answers to the questions screaming in my head? *What happened? Why don't you love me anymore?*

All of those came later, in the few short weeks before she deserted the new frontier and returned home. But now, as she climbed quickly from the car, I could only muster, "OK. I'll call you."

I'd spent hours gazing into that face, memorizing every curve and expression. I saw she wouldn't be looking forward to that call.

IS THIS WHO I THINK IT IS?

I kept staring at those words like you gaze at an abstract watercolor, hoping some significant form or design will emerge if you ponder long enough. After twenty years, how could I read between the lines of a one-line question? Was she really unsure about the identity of the author of the unexpected e-mail that dropped from her sky a few moments ago? Was she frightened or furious? Curious or excited?

I continued to puzzle over this one-sentence mystery, imagining the myriad of emotions, memories, and questions embedded within her enigmatic reply. The artist's vision failed to appear; her words still didn't reveal whatever secrets they concealed.

The observer's experiences and expectations too frequently shade the canvas, obscuring the painter's palette. As I searched for clues in the words on the screen, memories deflected my attention. Recollections of another lifetime.

CHAPTER 4

RUNNING

S unday afternoon in this dingy, cramped apartment seemed interminable. My new job didn't begin for a few weeks. I felt trapped
in this unfamiliar town that once represented promise and hope. The
demise of the dream transformed the Promised Land into a prison of
confusion and loneliness.

In the weeks since church I called Becky a few times, but she didn't
want to talk. I felt powerless to alter this horrible mess. I was indeed
stuck and hopeless as long the reality of denial still lurked beyond the
light of acknowledgement.

I decided a workout might provide an effective diversion. I didn't
really like running and the change to mile high elevation increased the
challenge of exercise. But I needed some activity to occupy the hours of
this endless day. I imagined, with partial sarcasm, that I might be lucky
and get hit by a car.

Questions, fears, and confusion cluttered my mind as I began to run.
I longed for the euphoria that sometimes accompanies intense exercise,
when everything slows down and thoughts clear. But the combination
of clamoring uncertainty and lack of acclimation to the altitude made
this anything but a pleasant and relaxing run. I resisted the urge to give
up and return home, choosing to struggle along, rather than face the
crushing loneliness.

Desperation overcame common sense and I impulsively ventured
into the heat of the July afternoon. I'd jog a few steps and stop, hands

on knees, gasping in the thin air. I trudged along, finding no rhythm in the exercise and no relief from the confusion clattering in my heart.

What happened to the dream? We planned to explore the New World together, sharing the excitement of a magnificent adventure as we created our perfect new life. Now I plodded slowly toward a bleak, uncertain future. I began to comprehend the terrible choice I'd made and the price I was going to pay for running from the light.

As I shuffled along the empty sidewalk, I wondered about a destination. I'd done minimal exploring of my new surroundings, but I recalled the little church and estimated it might be four or five miles away. I strained to keep moving, huffing and puffing, running from the loneliness and despair.

Finally! I saw the deserted church building in the distance. Hot, thirsty, and ready to quit, I stumbled to the side of the building and collapsed in the shade. After a few moments, my head cleared a bit and I noticed a garden hose. I rinsed my head and slurped greedily at the cool, bubbling stream. Soaked and refreshed, I sat in the shade and watched the traffic. I leaned back, pressed my head against the cool bricks and pondered the craziness of the past months.

Looking back, I marvel that this location provided a bit of shade and a drink of cool water. I didn't recognize then that I'd accidentally discovered *the* place to seek the peace that eluded me as I chased it madly everywhere else. The comfort I sought awaited, just like the cool water from that garden hose. I simply needed to pick it up.

I tried to calm my mind but the same thoughts kept crashing around. Why? What happened? I had not imagined this outcome, completely alone in the New World. Should I go back? Can't do that. But how could I go forward alone with no direction?

I noticed the sign in front of the church near the road.

Sunday Worship:	9:30 A.M. and 6:30 P.M.
Sunday School:	10:45 A.M.

Strange. I never considered church on Sunday night. Church happened on Sunday morning. Who went to church on Sunday evening?

I began to trudge slowly toward home. I wasn't really physically tired, but I lacked the mental energy to make myself start running again. "Who cares about this stupid workout anyway?" I grumbled to myself.

Finally I returned to the barren tomb of an apartment that now passed for "home." A long, cool shower felt good. I wished I could wash away the pain and loneliness as easily as the sweat. Out of the shower, and the dilemma remained. I still faced an interminable Sunday evening. The walls seemed to close around me as panic overwhelmed my efforts to contain it. I couldn't imagine one more night by myself in this strange place. All of my other emotions faded in the face of desperation. I had to do something. I needed someone to know I was here, to care about my fear and isolation.

I remembered that the church sign announced a service at 6:30 in the evening. I recalled the minister, the one who reminded me of an old friend. Maybe he would talk to me. At least it would be something to do, a way to fill the fearsome void of empty time.

Singing. That's mostly what happened in this Sunday night church gathering. Familiar songs, though I hadn't attended church since high school. Someone selected a hymn and everyone sang accompanied simply by a piano.

About fifty people were scattered in the first few rows; apparently only hard-core religious types attended church twice on Sunday. These folks appeared to know each other well. The person choosing the song often requested prayer or shared a significant experience. They discussed intimate issues openly, often with a good deal of emotion. Obviously these people spent time together and were involved in each other's lives. They felt safe here.

I sat alone in back, clearly an outsider, fighting the urge to leave. Instead of comforting me, their relaxed familiarity and my self-imposed isolation enhanced my loneliness and reinforced my identity as a stranger in a strange land. Church was simply one more place of isolation where nobody understood the fear that haunted me.

Later I'd learn something about the peace and support available among these people. I'd understand what this evening gathering meant to the small group singing and talking together. I'd even learn to be part of what happened here, to come on Sunday night and just let the presence of God and His people lift me up.

But that night I couldn't appreciate what transpired before me. Observing their cozy little warm-fuzzy-fest only enhanced my pain. Why should they float in peacefulness while I drowned in despair? Why were they surrounded by friendship while I sat alone and miserable and hopeless?

What brought them here to sing songs they'd probably sung a hundred times before? Why would someone stand in front of this group, share their fears and concerns, and ask everyone to sing a particular hymn?

Nothing I witnessed made any sense to me, and the lack of understanding made me feel even more alienated. I wondered why I came in the first place.

The minister who reminded me of a friend from home wasn't even there. I hoped to speak with him, and I picked his day off. I guess I didn't realize that ministers got Sundays off, since they didn't work during the rest of the week. Anyway, a pinch-hitter led this service. He seemed nice enough, and these people apparently knew and felt comfortable with him.

But why wasn't the other guy here? I had convinced myself I'd try to talk to him. I sensed the beginnings of a connection, a reason to trust him. He seemed pretty approachable, and maybe he'd spend a few minutes with me. Maybe a minister would be able to help, or at least would fill a portion of this one long, lonely evening. But he wasn't here tonight, and the imaginary dialogue I'd rehearsed in my car was falling apart.

I watched this new guy intently. His demeanor was friendly and sincere as he listened to the exchange. Most of the elements I expected in a regular church service seemed absent, but the substitute minister spoke for a few moments, uttering meaningless words about foreign notions that couldn't ease the haunting unrest. I thought he'd be OK to talk to. I had to do something; I couldn't just go back to that bleak, lonely apartment.

Everyone gathered outside after the service, the regulars in small groups sharing the familiar talk of people who knew each other well. I stood in the shadows, feeling more alone than ever as everyone else laughed and hugged while I hid and suffered. I watched the minister, waiting for a chance to catch him alone. Each time one person walked away, someone else stopped to chat. Approaching this guy alone appeared impossible.

At last, people began drifting to their cars, making arrangements to go for coffee while I stood apart, desperately awaiting my opportunity. The last group left him and he moved toward his own car. I wanted to just run into the night. Why would this stranger want to spend time with me anyway?

I almost turned away, but fear and desperation overcome embarrassment. I walked toward him, arriving just as he opened his car door. I stuck out my hand awkwardly.

"Hi, I'm Rich."

"Hello, I'm Hank. I saw you during the service."

"Yeah. Um—do you have some time to talk?"

Indecision flashed across his face. He anticipated a quiet evening at home with his own family or a pleasant time with friends. He'd completed his day, and I suddenly dropped from nowhere and asked to extend it.

"Right now?" He wanted to put it off, and I almost replied *No, that's OK, maybe some time when it works better for you.* I just could not face going home alone. I'd taken the first step, reached out, and I needed to grab something.

"Yeah, if you can. I'm having a pretty tough time, and I really don't know where else to turn. I need to talk to somebody, if it's all right."

Eternity balances on the small moments God uses to modify the course of a life. We're not usually aware of it at the time, but occasionally a left rather than right, yes instead of no, can alter all that follows. Frequently such choices seem simple and apparently innocuous, but you look back at such a moment and shake your head in wonder at what might have been if the coin had flipped differently. Life-altering episodes usually aren't the anticipated epic events that in retrospect really aren't so important.

This guy probably encountered numerous people "wanting to talk." I'll bet he frequently weighed the urgency of a particular request, whether he should honor his own plans and family life, and when a situation required him to change his course and spend time with someone in need.

I don't know how he chose that evening—perhaps a waver in my voice or considerable experience reading troubled faces—but something made him decide that this appeal shouldn't be postponed. A total stranger walked up to him, and with a few words he somehow knew.

"OK. Can you wait a minute while I go inside and make a phone call?"

"Sure." I swallowed the impulse to say *please, don't change your plans. I can make it another time. No big deal. Really.*

On this night it was a big deal. I could not go on like this. I could not return to the deserted wasteland that now masqueraded as "home."

"OK. I'll be right back." This pinch-hit minister turned and walked back to the church to call whomever was expecting him, to say that on this particular night, I needed him more than they did.

IS THIS WHO I THINK IT IS?

Would she even know me after so much time and change? How does one answer the question, "Who are you?" Beyond the obvious stuff—name, rank, and serial number—which parts of me would tell someone from two decades ago, "Who it is?" What is it that makes me—me? And how did I become whatever that is?

Would she even recognize the person who sent the unexpected message that appeared in her Inbox this morning? How much have the events and choices of twenty years made us different people?

Is that what her question asked? Did she know my identity, but not whom I'd become?

CHAPTER 5

THE STEPS

See, I am sending an angel ahead of you to guard you along the way and to bring you to the place I have prepared.

—Exodus 23:20

The minister locked the church door behind him and walked to where I leaned on his car. While he made his call, I had plenty of time to feel self-conscious about jumping into this guy's evening.

"I hope I'm not messing you up," I mumbled. "We really could do this at a better time."

"No problem. It's a great evening—how about if we walk a bit while you tell me what's on your mind?"

A neighborhood of small, neat houses surrounded the church building. As we began our stroll, evening slipped away. The sun slowly disappeared behind the mountains and front yards were filled with small kids and parents preparing to put the summer day away. We walked quietly, partly because of the pleasant surroundings, but mostly because I had no idea what to say or where to begin. Attempts at small talk sputtered and lapsed into awkward silences. This entire idea suddenly seemed like a mistake. I began to think that I should just let this guy go home.

"So—are you one of the ministers here?" I asked cleverly. "I was here a couple of weeks ago, and I saw a different leader."

"No," he replied. "My name is Hank. I'm the pastor of a church in Loveland, and we occasionally cover for each other during vacations and business trips. The preacher you heard was my friend Al."

"Oh." Great. One mystery resolved, and the conversation drifted into uneasy silence again. We walked a while longer, strained comments about yards and kids interspersed with a tense quiet so misplaced on this calm, warm evening. All I wanted was someone to talk to, and now I couldn't think of anything to say!

After a few blocks, Hank said softly, "Rich, you seem really troubled. What's going on?"

I hesitated. What should I say? How could I even begin to explain the mess I'd created? The confusion made no sense to me—how could I possibly convey the chaos of my life to a complete stranger?

Slowly, haltingly, I began to tell him of my struggles during the last couple of years—bad decisions, messed-up career, failed marriage, my mom's death. I mentioned Becky, but I wasn't sure how much to say, or maybe I had no idea what to say.

I gained momentum. As we wandered through this quiet neighborhood, I wandered through my thoughts, fears, dreams, disappointments, guilt, and loneliness. Hank commented or asked an occasional question, but mostly he just listened as I poured out my tangled, self-constructed predicament. Dusk descended; families abandoned sidewalks and yards and retreated inside.

At the time, I thought it strange that so little of my narrative involved Becky. I related the whole sad tale and only mentioned her character in an epilogue tossed in at the end of the book, an interesting afterthought but not really a chapter in the novel.

Interesting how things turn out, often so differently from our plans. I thought I needed to talk about Becky. Turns out, I really needed to open my life, recognize the emptiness, and begin to seek lasting and meaningful significance to fill the void. But I couldn't initiate that quest until I first understood that I *needed* to search.

In a book called *In Search of the Miraculous,* P. D. Ouspensky wrote that we are all in prison but we don't realize it, and as long as we don't recognize the cell, we're stuck there. The first requirement for escape is to acknowledge confinement. You have to see the bars for what they are before you can begin the process of removing them.

My journey along those peaceful streets comprised the very first baby-steps on a much more significant—and difficult—journey toward recognizing that I existed in prison and that I didn't want to live there any longer. It would be a long time, a lot of painful learning, before I got a handle on what that meant.

It would be much longer before I accepted that I could discover a key to the jail that confined me. In fact, I eventually learned that the door was locked from the inside and that I had always owned a get-out-of-jail-free card.

I eventually discovered that the significance I sought was just like the water from that garden hose earlier in the day. Cool and refreshing, right in front of me, yet I suffered with heat and thirst. The door to my personal jail had always been open, but I couldn't see it, and I couldn't walk through an invisible door, so I remained locked within my own fears and disappointments.

"Adam, where are you?" When the first man heard God calling to him in the cool of the evening, he hid in shame. Even after their disobedience, God sought out His creatures, still wanting to walk with them in the beauty of the garden. And even though they could clearly hear God's call, they hid from Him.

On that cool Colorado evening, I heard a call as hushed as the murmur of the breeze. As the traffic noises faded, and we walked in the stillness, I heard—no, I *felt*—God's call to me.

"Rich, where are you?"

I didn't recognize it that night. Clamoring despair so overwhelmed my mind, my heart, and my soul that I could scarcely hear anything else. But for just that brief moment, as the world around me became calm, so did the world within. For just that brief moment I heard and I *felt*, the peaceful, patient voice of God inviting me to walk with Him in the Garden. I couldn't identify it, I didn't understand it, and I had no idea what I experienced in the tranquility of those quiet streets. It would be a while before I understood that God had been relentlessly calling to me all along.

"Rich, where are you?"

God was inviting me to step through the prison door, to leave behind the doubt, fear, confusion, and loneliness that locked me behind their walls. I didn't consciously recognize the invitation, because His message was obscured by the internal commotion that disrupted our peaceful stroll. I didn't know yet that God was speaking to me. But my heart felt it—a small voice, a whisper as faint as the rustle of leaves in those Sunday evening trees, calling me to something different, something better.

"Rich, where are you?"

Hank asked me some simple questions as we meandered aimlessly along now-deserted sidewalks. What do you think brought you to this church? What do you believe about God? Do you know who Jesus is?

I offered intelligent-sounding answers to Hank's questions. Jesus taught important, useful ideas. I did believe in God, though I didn't really know what difference any of that made or how this ill-defined faith impacted my life.

My spirit mirrored the nighttime darkness as we approached the church. We'd walked and talked for a couple of hours, and I was exhausted. Not tired, but weary and beaten down by this struggle with no apparent purpose and no end in sight. I slumped down on the steps, just plain drained to the bone.

As we talked into the night on those steps, I recognized that I needed something and that what I required surrounded me. Though I didn't realize it that night, I heard that small whisper of a voice, summoning me to—what? I wasn't sure whether prayer was real or some sort of hocus-pocus. After years of awful choices, I wondered if I even had any right to suddenly pray to a God I'd ignored for so long. With no understanding of its significance, I took the first step in a surrender that took far too long to conclude. I asked Hank to help me talk to God.

"God, I need You. I've done so much wrong, hurt so many other people, and lost everything in my world. My mom, my friends, Becky, they're all gone. Help me, God. Please, help me."

Hank spent a few minutes telling me about his personal relationship with Jesus, about the difference that relationship created in his life, about how Jesus made him free. As I listened to Hank's affirmation of Jesus' presence, I broke down, as though I'd been struggling to bear a great weight and I simply could not support it any longer.

"Jesus, I don't know You, but I'm so lost. Please, help me."

In that moment, it was just a bit easier to hear that quiet, patient voice.

"Rich, where are you?"

I still didn't comprehend the reality of that call. I didn't know what it meant, and a lot of pain and struggle still awaited. But on those church steps, in that calm Colorado night, I made the initial move toward the response that would eventually open the prison door.

"Here I am, Lord."

As we parted, Hank hugged me and told me to call Al, the regular pastor, as soon as possible.

The next day, I made an appointment with Al. Then I walked to a lumberyard and bought two pieces of 1 x 2 pine. I fashioned a small crude cross and hung it in my bedroom. I really didn't understand the incredible gift and sacrifice symbolized by the cross. But my simple project was a symbol, a reminder of Hank, a life-altering evening, the steps, and the beginning of a jailbreak that would take longer than I could ever imagine.

IS THIS WHO I THINK IT IS?

Had twenty years really passed since I sat on those steps?

I turned and gazed at that simple wooden cross on the wall behind me. No way to know the journey we'd travel together when I constructed it all those years ago.

She knew nothing about any of this. She put me on the path toward those steps, and she didn't know where that path had taken me.

She couldn't know about the years of searching to understand who God is and how He matters in my life. Or that I figured out that Jesus died for me so I didn't have to remain in the prison of my own doubts and fears. She couldn't know how difficult it was to finally let go of the mistakes and failures that defined me for so long. She couldn't know that I finally heard God's call to me.

"Rich, where are you?"

She didn't know anything about what happened to me during those twenty years.

How could I possibly explain?

CHAPTER 6

THE MONSTER
IN THE MIRROR

CAT scans. X-rays. MRI exams. No doubt remained, and doctors delivered the shocking diagnosis: spinal cord injury! Three shattered vertebrae in my neck created uncertain central nervous system damage. I asked everyone the same fearsome questions. Now what? What's going to happen? Will I ever be able to walk?

My initial condition offered little encouragement. Arm movements were slow and difficult to control, while my hands simply flickered and twitched. Voluntary muscles below my shoulders remained lifeless. Is the paralysis permanent? We just can't tell for sure, because we don't know how much the injury damaged your spinal cord. Right now there's a lot of swelling, and when that subsides, the situation could change. We'll have to wait and see what happens during the next few days.

Intensive Care became my new home, body firmly fastened to the bed, neck immobilized in traction. Five days later, a team of neurosurgeons fused the vertebrae, joining crushed and splintered bones with an assortment of metal plates and screws along with a chunk of bone transplanted from my hip.

I emerged from surgery encased in a "halo brace" to stabilize my neck while the fusion healed. This contraption surely descended from some medieval instrument of torture, a metal jacket attached to vertical rods that clamped to a metal ring around my head—my "halo." Four screws secured the halo to my head. It took some time to assimilate that little piece of information—the thing was screwed into my skull!

I'm sure I was informed about the brace prior to surgery, but I don't remember much about those days. As the fog of the anesthetic subsided, I gradually became acquainted with this primitive apparatus that served as an inflexible exoskeleton to lock my upper body solidly in one position. Not that I could move much anyway, but this device added profoundly to the discomfort and frustration. Those screws protruding from my head even made lying on a pillow uncomfortable.

I had to learn to live with my new halo, because we'd be together for four months. Thankfully, at that point I couldn't imagine the horrible implications of this new addendum to my damaged body.

Days became weeks as the initial shock of the accident gradually merged with the daily struggle of preliminary recovery. Physical therapists appeared, at first to help me sit upright after so many days of lying down, allowing my body to adapt to the decreased circulation that accompanies paralysis. Like the thousands of unanticipated adjustments that lurked on the path to recovery, this simple movement that I'd taken for granted until a few days before, became a difficult and painful obstacle.

Every time the therapists elevated my head even a few degrees, my blood pressure plummeted as my heart labored to compensate. Dizziness and nausea overwhelmed me, and I wondered if I would ever be able to sit up again. The therapists expressed confidence that my body would eventually adjust, but this seemingly small preliminary step required an incredible amount of time and effort.

First, they would slide me onto a "tilt table" and strap me down. Then they'd check my blood pressure, elevate the table ten or fifteen degrees, wait a few seconds, and quickly crank the table level before I fainted as my body struggled to acclimate. Over and over, day after day, I achieved nearly imperceptible progress. Fifteen degrees of elevation increased to twenty, ten seconds increased to fifteen.

I became convinced I would never "get better." I couldn't perceive any tangible possibility that this ponderously slow struggle could lead to anything resembling a meaningful life.

The therapists tried hard to be friendly and encouraging, and make the best of an awful situation. Jokes, sports, movies, they tried every topic and tactic to distract me from the dismal circumstances and create a more pleasant and personal relationship. I wasn't playing their game. I was miserable and had no intention of pretending otherwise. I couldn't see beyond the halo, the catheter, the orthopedic stockings, and this bed that had become my prison. I did everything possible to make sure everyone around me understood the hopelessness, and that efforts to help were pointless and doomed to fail.

I also lost my voice, making a bad situation even worse. The surgeon accidentally damaged a nerve to my right vocal chord, so in addition to the paralysis, I could speak only in a hoarse whisper. I really didn't want to talk to anyone anyway, but communication now required significant effort. I effectively used my inability to speak as a perfect excuse to refuse any sort of positive interaction with anyone. I became increasingly mired in despair and anger.

After a few days, the staff provided an oversized reclining wheelchair. Though awkward and heavy, its design allowed the nurses and therapists to lean me back when I got light-headed, which happened every few minutes. Actually, I just sat in the chair. My arms still produced minimal useful motion, and I couldn't begin to move this clumsy chair by myself. This behemoth became my first mode of transportation, a way for others to push me where they wanted me to go. This unwieldy contraption symbolized my life, because it certainly had nothing to do with going where I wanted to go—nowhere.

Day followed dismal day as I made teeny-tiny bits of improvement that mostly felt like no progress at all. I moved from Intensive Care to a medical unit to recover from the surgery. I needed to reach the point of being "medically stable" which meant that immediate danger subsided and I didn't require IV medication or intensive nursing assistance. Then I transitioned to a rehabilitation unit to begin the arduous process of learning to live inside my damaged, ruined body.

A routine emerged. The rehab unit required daily physical therapy, so each morning an aide arrived in my room and lifted me into my chair. We'd check out at the nurses' station, then head down the hall and onto an elevator. Down four floors and through a maze of halls twisting and turning through the basement, our daily trek finally terminated in the waiting area of the PT gym.

A few weeks after my injury, the aide appeared after breakfast to fetch me. Same now-predictable process—he loaded into the bulky chair, then we took that familiar route to the basement waiting area. Quite by accident, he parked my chair near a full-length mirror. I didn't notice at first, but then a movement caught my eye. I saw the mirror slightly to the left, not directly in front of me but still within the limited field of vision created by the brace that prevented me from turning my head. At first, the reflection didn't register. It took a moment to realize the image in the mirror was—ME!

I stared in horror at the ghost gazing back at me through sunken, glazed eyes. He slumped limply in a large, leather wheelchair. Clothes appeared to hang from his emaciated skeleton. The feet pointed at odd angles like those of a rag doll carelessly arranged. His hair was uncombed and greasy and he hadn't shaved in several weeks. His skin looked a pale, chalky white. The ghastly specter evoked memories of grainy, black-and-white pictures from Nazi concentration camps, an empty half-alive stare that looks but doesn't really see.

And the halo brace! Screws protruded from his head, every bit like the Frankenstein monsters from those shadowy old movies. The creature might have escaped his shackles in some secret basement laboratory, the wretched result of a mad experiment gone horribly wrong.

I stared, gradually assimilating details of the shocking spectacle. Fascination faded to disbelief and then terror as I began to comprehend my link to the gruesome image. I moved my right arm as much as I could, like a child might do to verify that the reflection in the mirror was really connected to him. Sure enough, the monster's arm flopped across his body as well. That pathetic, half-human phantom was ME!

I'd never actually seen the halo brace. I guess I'd developed some sort of mental image of the awkward apparatus that immobilized my lifeless body, but I hadn't really considered the appearance of this horrific contraption. I certainly wasn't prepared for the ghastly image staring lifelessly back at me like some mistaken merger of man and mechanism. I wanted to escape from the pitiful, subhuman specter, but of course I couldn't move.

I couldn't run, couldn't walk, couldn't push the chair, couldn't even turn away. That monster remained right there in front of me, and I was powerless to evade his ghostly gaze. I couldn't even make him stop glaring at me. As fearsome as the apparition appeared, I couldn't force myself to squeeze my eyes shut and make him disappear.

I screamed in horror, or I did what passed for screaming with my hoarse whisper of a voice. No one heard my nearly silent wail, so I banged my arms in frustration on the sides of the chair. The spasmodic movements were the only volitional actions I could generate to attract attention and express my fear and anger.

Eventually one of the aides came to investigate the commotion. "Get me out of here," I rasped. "Take me back to my room." He didn't realize the source of my distress, but he pivoted the chair and we headed back toward the elevator. As we turned away, I got one last glimpse of the monster in the mirror. I croaked another horrified moan.

Back in my room, no one could console me or make sense of what had upset me. "Just leave me alone! Go away! Let me alone!" I whispered through tears.

"What's wrong?" asked Julie, my nurse. "What happened?"

I didn't want to talk. Didn't want to tell her about the monster, about the horror of the frightening image that confronted me, about the embarrassment of finally realizing what others saw when they looked at me. I just wanted to turn off the lights and hide my pathetic remnant of a person in darkness. "Everyone, just get out. LEAVE ME ALONE!" Now I was begging, "Please, turn off the lights and go away."

In the cool darkness of the hospital room, I cried. How could all of this have happened? The entire period since the accident drifted past in a horrible, surreal haze—ambulance, emergency room, Intensive Care, surgery, recovery. Weeks passed in a fog of pain, sleep, and drugs, until the days had little definition and time either passed or not. It didn't much matter. The shock of the entire episode blurred the distinction between reality and some sort of bizarre nightmare. I acted in the dream, aware, but not really. The whole dreadful muddle seemed like a struggle to awaken from a dream within a scene in a bad movie.

But in that dark room, the fog began to lift. That ghastly, half-dead reflection wasn't a character in a scary dream or the product of a drug-induced hallucination. The screws in my head, the chair that trapped me, the feet that didn't appear to be connected to the legs I couldn't see or feel—that pitiful fabrication of some demented imagination is what remained of ME. I had become that gaunt, slumped, pathetic-looking monster. I cried.

I sat where they left me, facing toward the window of my room. The blinds were mostly closed, and I stared blankly at the window. I heard the door open quietly behind me. "Rich?" Julie whispered. "What can I do?"

"Nothing," I murmured. "Please, leave me alone." The door closed again, and I was alone.

Much of the day passed like that. The nursing shift changed and the night nurse, Angela, came by to try her luck. She took a lighter approach. "All right, buck-o, what in the hell happened? Let's get back in the game."

Silence.

The door closed again. I sat alone.

I cried, stared at the blinds, and cried some more. I should have been out of the chair and back in bed a long time ago. I felt dizzy, light-headed, and nauseous. I struggled to breathe, and my back ached. But I couldn't move, couldn't turn the chair or call for help if I'd wanted to. I was just there. Helpless and alone.

I heard the rustle of the door once more. No idea how long I'd been there. Didn't care. I sighed, anticipating another attempt to break through and get me to talk. Who had they sent this time to convince the freak to respond?

The room became dark as the door closed again. Just the dim light from the hallway crept through from under the door. Silence for a few moments, but somehow a different quality permeated the room. A small bit of peace had settled in the shadows.

"Rich." Spoken so softly, I almost felt it more than heard it. "Rich, may I come in?"

Tears flooded my eyes again. I'd first heard that quiet, reassuring voice more than six years ago when Becky invited me to church. I noticed a peaceful, settling sort of quality about it then, although I hadn't sorted that out from all of the other thoughts and emotions that whirled in my head on that long-ago day. I listened to that calm tone nearly every Sunday since, helping me begin to quiet the turmoil in my heart and guide me patiently toward an understanding of the personal God I'd come to know.

He stood by my bed frequently during these last terrible days and weeks, listening to expressions of pain and anguish, helping me to remember I wasn't alone in any of this. Many times he left me late in the evening with the powerful, calm assurance that, when all else crashed down about me, Jesus stood with me and held me in His arms. He constantly reminded me that Jesus understood my fear, knew the pain and would help me find a way to somehow get through another long, lonely hospital night.

"Al," I whispered. "Yeah, please come in."

He crossed the room and stopped beside me. I could hear him there, and then I felt his hand on my shoulder. He stood beside me in dark silence, and we stared at the blinds for a few moments. I cried and he held me awkwardly, avoiding the screws, and cradled my head as the fear and pain gushed out. The emotion of this miserable day completely overwhelmed me and the terror of the past weeks seemed to rip at my soul. I sobbed uncontrollably, but I was no longer alone.

Finally, I couldn't cry anymore. I couldn't wipe my own runny nose, so Al got a cool washcloth and gently cleared away a day's worth of tears. I took a long, deep breath and looked at him for the first time. "You've had a pretty rough day," he said. "The nurses are really worried about you. Is it OK if Angela comes in and we'll get you back in bed and get something for you to eat?"

"Yeah." I sighed. "That would be good."

Angela and an aide entered quietly, afraid to break some sort of spell that seemed to hang in the room. I was helped from the uncomfortable chair, lifted into bed, legs arranged, shoes off, another cool cloth for my face. Dinner waited, and Al helped me eat a little. The clean sheets felt good—at least, what I could feel of them. Then everyone left. "Do you want to talk about it?" Al asked.

I told him about the monster in the mirror and the horrible panic, about finally understanding what I had become. How could I ever go outside the room again? How could people even tolerate such a terrifying figure? Why had no one told me about my freakish appearance?

"I can't live like this. This cannot be what God wants anyone to be. I need to die—that *thing* in the mirror needs to die. That can't be me. What happened to *me*? Where did I go?"

Al and I talked for a long time that evening. We spoke about the embarrassment of feeling like some strange creature that belonged in a circus sideshow rather than in my body. We talked about the last weeks, the blur of time that had passed yet hadn't, about the fear that I'd never get better, about who—or what—I was in this lifeless skeleton of a body with the Frankenstein screws in my head. I asked the same questions again and again, "What happened to ME? Where did I go? How can that monster in the mirror be *me*?"

At one point, Al went to the bathroom and came back with a hand mirror. "You need to take another look at yourself."

I recoiled in horror. How could he possibly imagine I'd want to see that monstrous reflection again? But he persisted, gently telling me I needed to take a better look, a calmer look. I needed to see *me* in the mirror. After a long time and a lot of angry, fearful refusing, I agreed. Slowly, Al brought the small hand mirror up until it was in front of my face.

I closed my eyes as the reflection appeared before me, then opened them a little as though a game of hide-and-seek would make the image easier to regard. I saw a hollow face with a sallow complexion. The eyes darted back and forth, brief glimpses before looking away and back again. I noticed the same scraggly beard and unkempt hair I'd seen earlier. And then I saw them—the screws and the metal halo they held in place around my head. I squeezed my eyes shut tightly and waited a few moments before I found the courage to open them again.

The halo of silver-colored metal hung suspended about half an inch away from my head. I could see two of the screws embedded in my forehead about an inch above and outside of each eyebrow. I knew there were two more screws in the back, covered by hair. I knew because twice each day a nurse painfully cleaned the area around all four screws to prevent infection.

I stared with some combination of fascination and disbelief. How had my life come to this? How could THAT be ME? Al steadied the mirror for several moments and allowed the image to hang there in front of me. I gazed in silence at the horrible shadow staring back at me with those sunken, glazed eyes. Who is that? Where did *I* go?

Al must have seen the questions on my face, because he said quietly, "Rich, you're in there."

"Where?" I whimpered. "I can't . . . that can't . . . I don't see me there."

"Rich, you're in there," he repeated. "Inside. You are not what you see in the mirror. What you see right now is pain and sorrow and a catastrophic injury that's going to need a long time to heal. You see fear and loss and grief. You see a brace that looks horrible because of the horrible job it has to do. You see all of that, and you think you're seeing *you*.

"But all of that stuff isn't you. It's stuff, awful stuff, but it's all on the outside, and it'll all go away. Even the brace—four months is an awfully long time to have such a terrible contraption attached to you, but it'll go away. None of what you see right now is *you*. But you're in there, underneath the unimaginable things that have happened to you."

I asked him to pray with me. Al was good about that. He was a pastor who loved God with all his heart but didn't just drop "Jesus" into a situation as though that would make it all better and you never should have been sad or scared in the first place because you should just need to have enough faith. Now he prayed with me, and as he prayed, he also reminded me I wasn't alone. He laid the mirror down, took my paralyzed, limp hand in his hands and prayed.

"Lord Jesus, be here with us. Rich is really scared right now, Father, and he has every reason to be scared. A terrible thing has happened and Rich doesn't even know where he is anymore. He looks in the mirror and he can't find himself, and instead he sees a hideous, frightening reflection of evil.

"Father, hold Rich in Your hand right now. Let him know that Your arms surround him tonight, that he's safe, and that he has not gone anywhere. Let him know that he's right here, and that You know all about his battles. Remind him that Jesus felt the fear, knows the pain, and understands what it means to feel lost and alone. Father, help Rich to sense the powerful presence of Jesus in this room right now through Your Spirit.

"And Father, grant to Rich Your peace in this moment. He faces a long and difficult road, but help him to know he doesn't have to travel that road tonight. Help him to let go, fall into Your arms, and be at peace.

"Father, I ask this, for Jesus' sake. Amen."

The room that was filled with so much turmoil all day was unexpectedly quiet, still and peaceful. This dreadful situation wasn't suddenly all OK. But it was somehow OK in that moment. Al and I talked a while longer. He reminded me that there were no magic, easy answers to this dilemma and that I'd likely encounter frightful images again. But he asked if I could let the peace in the room settle over me, just for tonight.

"Yeah," I whispered. "I'm really tired. I'll be all right. Thanks."

He smiled. "I'll be back tomorrow and we'll see what monsters we need to talk about then."

"Can't wait." He squeezed my hand and turned to leave.

"Wait. Take the mirror. I'm liable to drop it and cause a run of bad luck."

We laughed quietly together. I've always believed those laughs were gifts from God.

Al was sure right about one thing, my journey didn't get magically easier that night. God never promised every season of life would be easy. He did promise we would never have to face any situation alone. That doesn't make it easy, but it DOES offer hope.

Hope provides a permanent solution to a temporary problem. The hope God offers isn't the sort of wishful thinking so prevalent at birthday celebrations. "I *hope* I get a new bike" confuses hope with some sort of superstitious yearning. I *hope* my team wins the big game. I refuse to wash my lucky jersey because I *hope* it'll bring good luck. That's not God's hope.

God bestows, through His grace, the kind of hope that might be more accurately described as "expectation." God doesn't promise that I can wish for His peace; He promises that I can expect to receive it. God's hope isn't based on wishes or luck or maybe. God's hope implies certainty rooted in grace and love.

How can I know with absolute assurance that Jesus will jump into the hole with me? Because He already did it when He left the glory of heaven to live among us. How can I know that He knows the escape route from my particular trap? Because He already escaped from the deepest, darkest trap imaginable—death on the cross, and even death couldn't defeat Him.

Only one thing is required—that I turn around, face Him, and acknowledge my dependence upon His presence. I simply need to stop running toward the shadows and face the light.

That night I felt the power and hope and the presence of Jesus. I knew He stood with me, walked beside me, and even carried me when I needed it. The palpable tranquility that filled my hospital room that night drove away the fear of the monster in the mirror.

In a moment when I couldn't see a way out, God provided. He didn't solve the problem or make the pain disappear. But He did give me what I needed at that moment. He made that night, at the end of an awful day, a night of peace.

I wish I could proclaim that I never gave up again, never got frustrated or fearful, never forgot to lean on God's promises. I wish I could say that after that night I always remembered that Jesus knew the pain and the fear and would always be with me. I wish I had been able to carry the peace of that night through the difficult days and weeks ahead.

I wish I could say I claimed God's hope and never again lapsed into despair, but I didn't yet fully understand His offer. I wished for a miracle to remove the monster; I didn't hope with certainty for the ultimate peace God promised.

I wished, but in fact I continued to give up and get angry and frustrated. Time and again I found myself at the end, lost and alone. No where to turn, no idea how to get out of this one.

And every time, God provided. Not in an easy way, not an end to the pain. But Jesus was always with me. Somehow He helped me summon the strength to go on when I was certain I couldn't go any farther. Whenever I could find no escape from the fear, God provided.

IS THIS WHO I THINK IT IS?

People hardly notice the small scars on my forehead where those screws were attached. The scraggly beard's gone, along with most of the hair. Less hair, more weight, so I guess it all balances out.

I wondered how she would have reacted to the "monster in the mirror?" Would she have been repulsed? Would she run away from the fearful freak with screws in his skull? Would she have been haunted by the same nightmares that invaded my sleep for so many years?

I wondered if she remembered Al? Does she recall the day she invited me to church and saved my life?

CHAPTER 7

HEAVEN

S pinal Cord Injury denotes varying degrees of damage to the nerves in the spinal cord. The body's amazing design incorporates a number of protective safeguards, and often this extremely serious injury isn't immediately medically life threatening. Even when paralysis prevents most voluntary movements, life-sustaining automatic functions continue. Injuries high in the neck sometimes create breathing issues and cause dependence on a ventilator, and comprehensive treatment addresses a long list of other potentially critical concerns. But SCI is primarily chronic and forces adjustments to just about every aspect of life.

In the weeks and months following my injury, I encountered medical challenges in nearly every part of my body: breathing, circulation, skin care, nutrition, bladder/bowel, kidneys, even keeping my toenails healthy. An entire range of physical concerns I'd taken for granted during the first thirty-six years of my life suddenly required care and attention.

I even had to practice coughing! I learned to be wary of minor infections, illnesses, cuts, and many other seemingly insignificant ailments. All sorts of everyday problems that were merely annoying just a few weeks ago, suddenly became serious issues.

My injury involved the sixth and seventh cervical and the first thoracic vertebrae, so my SCI was classified as C6-C7-T1. Spinal cord nerves in that location control arm and hand functions. An injury slightly higher might have completely paralyzed my hands, while damage just a little lower might not have affected my hands and arms at all.

My injury caused nearly total paralysis below my chest, but I retained minimal arm use. Over time, I've been fortunate to regain nearly unrestricted movement of my arms and some use of my hands. I utilize normal utensils to do things such as eat and brush my teeth, and with minor modifications, I can write and use a computer.

But in the weeks after my accident, I couldn't move around independently at all, couldn't even roll myself over in bed, so to avoid bedsores someone had to turn me every two hours. I pretty much stayed wherever someone left me. And since I still found little motivation to do anything that wasn't absolutely necessary, I tended to stay in bed a lot. I got up for physical therapy in the morning, but as soon as I returned to my room, I asked to be transferred back to bed. The ritual repeated each afternoon. I complained about pain or dizziness, grumbled about my dependence on others, and feigned exhaustion—I'd create any excuse to get out of that uncomfortable chair. Despite efforts to encourage me, this routine resulted in a complete lack of exercise or any other movement at all.

Restricted movement contributed to constrained, shallow breathing which didn't efficiently clear my lungs. I couldn't cough effectively because the injury affected my diaphragm. Nurses and therapists tried hard to encourage deep breathing and coughing exercises, but I didn't put much effort into this important therapy. Over a few weeks' time, the combination of my sedentary existence and inadequate breathing created a dangerous situation: I developed pneumonia.

Pneumonia's nothing to mess with even if you're relatively healthy. For someone who doesn't move around much, the infection can lead to serious complications, even the risk of death. I wasn't completely aware of the danger, but I vaguely recall significant concern from the doctors and nurses.

A pulmonary specialist joined my medical team. Every two hours respiratory technicians inserted a tube into my nose that sucked fluid from my lungs. IV's delivered multiple powerful antibiotics and x-ray technicians appeared frequently to check the progress of the illness, but nothing seemed to effectively mitigate my symptoms. While I didn't fully recognize the implications of the increased attention, I was clearly in peril.

As the infection progressed, I became increasingly lethargic. Despite the best efforts of the medical team, I spiraled downward. Later I learned that I lapsed into a kind of semi-coma.

I opened my eyes in total stillness, none of the hospital noises to which I'd become accustomed. I lay on my right side, and I couldn't see anything. I moved my eyes from side to side, but darkness obscured my surroundings. I felt as though I floated in a totally black, open space, alone in a dark void. I didn't try to move, didn't try to speak, just lay there and rested in peaceful silence.

It was so completely still. I wasn't afraid, even though I could see and hear nothing to help me orient myself. Peace, that's what it was. It felt like a palpable peace had settled around me. I closed my eyes for a moment, or maybe for a long time.

When my eyes opened again, the same calm, serene blackness. I glanced toward my feet and perceived a vague shadow of an image. Someone stood beside me, a presence almost felt more than seen. I waited in the perfect tranquility, and as my eyes adjusted to the darkness, I discerned a faint outline. A man, standing very near, head bowed. Even in the silence, I could sense the man was praying. I closed my eyes again, for a moment or a lifetime.

He's still there. No sound, no movement, just standing there immersed in prayer. Muted details, just the silhouette of this figure standing motionless beside me, head bowed, surroundings so calm I can almost hear his thoughts. Peaceful, quiet, and dark, just this shadowy form hunched over me.

I waited, quiet, serene, and contented, no desire to do anything or say anything. Everything seemed restful, somehow just as it was supposed to be. I couldn't determine who stood next to me, somehow certain there was no need to know. It was just right to be here, to just be in the tranquility and peace surrounding me. I was exactly where I belonged. I knew I was safe, as though love had come alive, wrapped its arms around me, and held me securely in this place of peacefulness.

It's Jesus! Jesus is standing beside me. This must be Heaven, this space of such perfect peace and calm. I've died. I'm in Heaven, and Jesus is standing beside me, praying over me. No fear, no questions, just tranquility and calm. No emotions—not excitement, not wonder, not sadness. Everything here is just filled with a sense of serenity; it's all just as it's supposed to be. So quiet, so safe, no more pain, no more fear. I took a deep breath, smiled and closed my eyes.

Heaven.

Sunlight streamed through the open blinds of the hospital room. I couldn't raise my hands to shield my eyes, so I blinked several times until I adjusted to the brightness. "Rich, you're awake." I recognized Julie's voice. "Wow, you had a tough night. Everyone was really worried about you. It's good to see you this morning."

I didn't respond. Frowning, I tried to get oriented and banish the confusion. Oh, yeah. Hospital, injury, pneumonia. I didn't remember going to bed last night. Julie must have noticed the frown.

"You've been a little out of it for a couple of days. How are you feeling?"

I muttered something, still trying to get my bearings.

She continued, "The docs came in early this morning, but you didn't budge. They said your lungs look better and your fever's down a bit. Seems like things are looking up!" she said in her cheery nurse voice.

"What happened last night?" I whispered.

"Well, when I came to work this morning the night nurses said you had a really bad evening, coughing, high fever, never really responded no matter what they tried. The doc changed antibiotics again, but they said things were getting worse. They talked about moving you back to Intensive Care.

"You apparently were quite agitated, even though you didn't wake up. Sweating, moaning, just not a happy camper at all." She paused. "Angela remembered a couple of weeks ago when you got so upset, and she called your pastor. She said he was at one of his kids' school events when she phoned, but he called back later in the evening. She explained what was happening, and he said he'd come over.

"I guess he got here pretty late, and he must have stayed here most of the night from the way Angela talked. Apparently you calmed down when he got here, and then he just stuck around."

I smiled. "So that's what it was," I whispered to myself.

"What?" Julie heard me murmur something.

"Nothing. It's OK."

Amazingly, and for no apparent reason, I did get better over the next few days. Therapists returned to my room, and we began anew the ordeal of getting upright, nearly passing out, lying down, and repeating the cycle. The pneumonia receded and cleared up, doubtless because the right antibiotic had finally been selected, or because I was lucky, or maybe just because. Or maybe there was another reason for my sudden recovery.

Al didn't come by for a couple of days. He'd called to check on me and found out I was improving. When he finally came through the door, I laughed. "Well, that's quite a change." He chuckled. "The last time I saw you we weren't sure you were going to make it. I'm so happy to see your smiling face."

"So," I croaked. "Have you been doing any more cosmic travels impersonating Jesus?"

He looked at me as though I was still in a drug-induced haze, so I laughed and told him the story. I ended with, "I thought you were Jesus."

He smiled, looked at the floor, and shuffled his feet in a feigned "aw-shucks" pose that made both of us giggle. "Yeah, well, don't let it get around."

Another laugh shared between friends, another gift from God.

When I opened my eyes in the quiet darkness and believed Jesus stood beside me in Heaven, I was completely at rest. No fear, no questions, no need to understand, just safe and loved beyond anything I'd ever experienced. This wasn't some sort of mystical near-death experience. I emerged from the depths of a semi-coma, saw the dim outline of my friend praying beside my bed, and mistook him for Jesus. I was nowhere near Heaven; I was in Room 3057, which I am absolutely certain was about as far as possible from Heaven.

But I'm also absolutely certain that Jesus *was* in that room. No, I didn't see Him standing there; that was just Al. But Jesus was there, just as He was there when I fell, and just as He's been beside me every painful step of the way.

I failed to truly grasp the significance of that night until much later. At so many places in this journey, God offered His peace and rest. I might have held on to the quiet security that enveloped me as my friend prayed over me. I might have claimed the unquestioned sense that all was OK and moved forward with the knowledge that I wasn't alone, that God worked for good even in the horrible circumstances of my injury. I might have truly trusted Him and believed that He'd show me meaning in the midst of senselessness.

I might have done those things. Such an approach surely would have made the experience less painful and the loss easier to bear. Certainly that's how an inspirational movie would have proceeded.

But this wasn't a movie, and the real-life me wasn't ready yet to surrender the misery or let go of the struggle. I wasn't yet ready to walk (or, more accurately, to roll) through the door of my self-constructed prison and live in the freedom of God's grace and the hope that grace provides. I wasn't ready yet to trust that God was bigger than the hospital and the halo brace and the monsters that lurked in the shadows of my fear.

But even in the midst of clinging to the anxiety and refusing to consciously acknowledge the possibility of anything better, God gave me a glimpse of potential, and what was available to me just for the asking. I wasn't open yet to believing that good could be found in this terrible new life, and as a result, this important occurrence didn't provide the relief that might have been. But the experience was there, hanging out in the background, waiting for the right moment to step out and take its place in the tapestry of my life that God was so patiently and faithfully weaving.

In the face of unspeakable terror, I experienced the certain knowledge that Jesus stood beside me. Even if only for a moment, I felt the peace that accompanied that belief. I knew the reality of Jesus' presence, so certain there was no need to ask, "Is this who I think it is?" In the end, when I was finally ready, the power of that encounter would alter the course of my life.

IS THIS WHO I THINK IT IS?

As I continued to read and ponder, her seemingly meaningless question transformed itself, assuming significance and insight. I was starting to wonder if I even knew "who this is."

How would she react if I told her I once thought I was in Heaven? You have to be kind of careful with a story like that. Being paralyzed is bad enough; I don't want to end up on the psych ward!

I recalled wondering what Becky was doing while I was imprisoned in that hospital room. Her birthday was right before Valentine's Day.

I wondered what her birthday was like while I was struggling to survive.

How many more questions can possibly arise from this simple e-mail message?

CHAPTER 8

HAPPY VALENTINE'S DAY

I invested almost no effort in the therapy that would determine so much of the nature and course of my remaining life. I simply saw no reason to believe this horrible situation could ever improve.

Maybe I just waited for that miracle to provide a compelling ending to the movie screenplay. You wake up one morning and formerly life-less body parts magically begin moving, the paralysis disappears for no apparent reason, and it all turns out OK. I still operated in denial; this whole experience simply *couldn't* be real. And as long as I refused to face the situation honestly, I wasn't going to make the effort required to actually get better.

Much like that imaginary prison door I first encountered on the church steps, the injury trapped me behind walls of despair and denial. As long as I refused to confront those bars, I could never move beyond them. I was still committed to running from the light, and the fantasy of magic healing prevented me from facing reality and taking control of my future.

Movies and television foster unrealistic expectations. Complex mysteries dissolve into quick solutions, deadly diseases disappear miraculously, and everyone lives happily ever after. Even when the conclusions aren't the stuff of fairy tales, the dreadful events transpire in the darkness and then the movie ends. You finish your popcorn and head out the door and everything's just as you left it. The daily grind of a rehab unit, a cancer ward, or a hospice wouldn't comprise a setting for compelling television in which every plot line must tidily conclude within sixty minutes while still allowing time for commercials.

Many popular self-help programs feed the fantasy of the magic bullet. They'll sell you the instant formula for $19.95: follow the simple steps and you'll lose weight, make friends, or locate your soul mate quickly and easily. Twenty easy minutes a day for a few weeks will transform that flabby body into the toned, muscular, sexy image on the supermarket magazine cover. The power of positive thinking overcomes any malady or distress. Everything will be perfect if you just—whatever.

Religion isn't immune from this temptation to view the world through somewhat tinted lenses. Just have faith and God will make everything all right. He'll cure your disease, protect your family, bless your national goals, and bestow fortune and fame upon you. We'll even make sure God heals you, if you send a generous contribution to the toll free number on your screen.

Something unfortunate happened to you? Well, possibly you didn't pray correctly, or maybe your faith isn't strong enough to earn God's grace and favor. Or perhaps it's God's judgment, His punishment for those unforgivable sins; not the normal little slips we all make, but you know, those *real* sins for which God just has to zap you.

One of the pastors in my church recently revealed that he struggled for a time with clinical depression. He consulted doctors, received treatment, and worked his way through the problem. However, he told us that a common reaction among his religious friends was a sort of puzzled expression, followed by a question that went something like, "Depressed? How can you be depressed if you really have the victory of Jesus in your life?"

Unfortunately, life isn't a TV show, a movie, or the latest best-selling self-help book. Jesus never promised that His people would be immune from the evils of the world or that faithfully following Him guaranteed health, wealth, and security.

But our culture is awash with this quick-fix mentality, and I allowed myself to remain in its trap. Rather than approaching my situation from a long-term perspective, I didn't look past the depressing, no-hope hospital room. My friend Wally was one of the few visitors I allowed, and each time he appeared, we played a little game of counting my days in the hospital. We finally ended at one hundred forty seven days—twenty-one weeks! But as day sixty passed and Valentine's Day approached, I was going nowhere.

I failed to recognize the effects of my accident on others. It's terrible to watch helplessly while someone you love suffers with a debilitating injury or illness. Those close to me wrestled with their own fear, doubt, and guilt, but I couldn't see their pain through the fog of self-pity. My negative attitude made the experience even more difficult for friends and family.

My refusal to make any effort to get better caused a huge emotional drain on everyone who wanted to help me. I could have eased the stress for those who worried about and wanted the best for me, but I just couldn't perceive anything beyond the halo brace, the chair I couldn't move in, and the hospital that seemed more like a tomb from which I would never escape.

I managed to emerge a bit from this cloud of self-pity when my dad and his wife, Marje, announced plans to visit for Valentine's Day.

The shock of my injury, the interminable days in Intensive Care and surgery hit my dad especially hard. He struggled through a tough time about ten years earlier as my mom fought a losing three-year battle with lung cancer. Now he watched his oldest son lie paralyzed, strapped lifelessly into a bed for five days.

He dreaded the hospital/ICU environment. Painful memories haunted waiting areas, despair and helplessness lurked in rooms filled with trauma equipment. I cannot even imagine his terror when I awakened from surgery with that horrible halo brace screwed into my head.

Dad and Marje rushed to Fort Collins from their home near Portland the day after my accident, and remained until my condition stabilized following surgery. I realized how frightening the upcoming visit would be for Dad as he confronted my lifeless, emaciated body and freakish appearance. I knew he'd be devastated when he saw first-hand how little I'd progressed in more than two months.

After several weeks, I could only still sit upright for just a few minutes at a time. I decided I'd try to increase my sitting time so I could be out of bed for part of Dad's visit. I somehow imagined that slumping in that bulky chair might make the hospital environment and the image of my pathetic, gaunt, paralyzed body easier for him.

I started working to extend my wheelchair time. The process was unbelievably difficult; how could the simple act of sitting in a chair be so incredibly uncomfortable? I'd slouch, more or less upright, as long as possible until dizziness and nausea became unbearable. Then an aide would tip my chair back, and I'd struggle to breathe while allowing the spinning head and queasy stomach to abate.

A few minutes lying down, then upright, and repeat the agonizing cycle again and again until my body gradually adapted and I could tolerate sitting for slightly longer intervals. For the first time since the injury, I actually set an important goal for myself and worked toward achieving something positive.

I began to believe I might succeed, and I'd be able to sit up for a significant period of time when Dad arrived. I secretly felt a bit of pride in this small accomplishment. The advance that felt so significant and required so much effort seems trivial in hindsight, but in fact it wasn't trivial at all. Perhaps I'd turned a corner, and this first modest achievement would lead to more substantial gains. Maybe a light existed at the end of this long, dark tunnel, and possibly, just possibly, that light did not signal an approaching train.

Discouragement always lingered immediately beneath every tedious success, eager to supplant the satisfaction of accomplishment. After so much effort, I could remain upright and relatively comfortable for thirty short minutes. Then I'd be lifted into bed, groaning and complaining about my aching back and the impossibly slow improvement. Pain and frustration consistently screamed for attention and threatened to silence the whisper of painstaking progress.

Now that I actually worked toward a goal, transfers between bed and chair became more frequent. These initial signs of effort pleased nurses and therapists, so they encouraged me to get into the chair as often as possible. I suspect that the first hint of exertion also made me a little less disagreeable, which probably pleased them even more.

Initially, the lift from chair to bed required two attendants, but eventually, an efficient method evolved that one person could accomplish safely. As the originally unwieldy procedure became more manageable, even the nurses now could pivot me into bed by themselves. One morning I returned from my physical therapy session and sat in my room watching television for a few minutes before pressing the nurse's call button. Dad's visit was just a couple of days away, and I felt good about finally accomplishing something positive.

Julie appeared at the door with her usual cheery smile. Her personality suited this kind of work perfectly—calm and patient, committed to helping her seriously injured clients become healthy and productive. She brightened this prison-cell hospital room every time she entered. Her upbeat optimism seemed unaffected by my consistently unresponsive, pessimistic, angry approach to nearly everything and everyone. I really did appreciate her constant positive demeanor, though I seemed incapable of responding appropriately to her kindness.

"Ready to get back in bed?" She knew it was pointless to encourage me to remain in the chair a few minutes longer. I'd just whine and complain, so she avoided the negative interaction we'd rehearsed so often.

Julie moved my chair into position next to the bed, arranged my feet, and prepared for the transfer procedure she'd repeated dozens of times. She stood in front of me, wrapped her arms around the halo jacket that encased my upper body, and performed the lift-and-pivot scheme we'd developed. The maneuver worked well and she easily and smoothly hoisted me onto the mattress.

Except—when my backside landed on the bed, something unexpected occurred. I heard and felt a loud BANG and suddenly I felt an odd sensation. I still hadn't developed clear perceptions of function and sensation in my altered body, so I didn't realize exactly what had happened. But I knew immediately that something was wrong.

Julie still clasped her arms around me as we sprawled awkwardly on the edge of the mattress. Lying in bed with a cute young nurse may be the stuff of juvenile male fantasy, but the artificial laugh track clearly didn't fit this particular scene. She tried to reach for the call button without letting go of me, but it dangled off the foot of the bed beyond her grasp. She yelled for help. I still couldn't determine what was wrong, but her cries conveyed distress and urgency.

Two other nurses ran into the room, and I saw fear in their eyes. These people witnessed terrible events every day, and they usually remained pretty calm and collected. Whatever they observed stunned even these experienced, normally unflappable professionals. Their shocked expressions didn't arise from the spectacle of Julie and me wrapped around each other in a hospital bed.

One of the new arrivals immediately scurried for the call button to summon more help, while the other rushed to cradle my head with her hands and forearms. Julie finally climbed carefully from her awkward position on top of me. I remained quite close to the edge of the mattress, my legs dangling limply over the side. The fear reflected in her face clutched at me with an icy terror that squelched my urge to joke about our momentary embrace.

"What happened?" I croaked. The expression that flashed across her features reminded me of that ER nurse's face more than two months ago. She didn't want to tell me.

The cumbersome position in which I was trapped was becoming painful. Eleanor held my head and shoulders tightly, so my legs hanging off the bed twisted my body at an awkward angle. "What's wrong?" I repeated hoarsely. "This is really uncomfortable. Can you get my legs up on the bed?"

She hesitated. "Not right now," she almost whispered. "You need to lie still."

"Why? What's wrong?" What could possibly make them reluctant to move my already-paralyzed legs?

Finally, she delivered the shocking news. "It looks like your halo came loose."

"What? What does that mean? How could that happen?" The questions poured out faster than she could address them. How could that Frankenstein contraption become unfastened? It's screwed into my head! What does she mean—came loose? Is my skull broken or something?

Now I understood the emergency, the rush to secure my head, their refusal to move me. The surgeon originally estimated that healing required about four months, and the halo was designed to immobilize my neck and prevent further damage. What if the bones moved? Could the fusion break? What if the screws and plates that secured my shattered spine pulled loose? Had I damaged my spinal cord even more? How would this affect my chances for recovery?

How could this have happened?

I stared again at the stark white ceiling while the room buzzed with unseen activity. Nobody seemed to quite know what should happen next. Once again I strained to understand disembodied voices as people entered and talked quietly in small groups about this unanticipated accident. I choked on the too-familiar fear of unknown outcomes, waiting as the terror mounted for someone to explain what had occurred. But this time no face appeared to reassure me and no fog obscured the agonizing moments as I searched for answers on the ceiling.

I heard an announcement from the overhead speaker calling my surgeon's partner, another neurosurgeon—*STAT*! I knew enough hospital jargon to understand "STAT" meant he should respond quickly. They needed him right now.

The room eventually calmed a bit. People still came and went, talking in hushed voices, but the rush diminished. Eleanor still cradled my head and shoulders. She stood behind me where I couldn't see her, but finally the commotion subsided enough that she could hear my frightened whisper. "What's happening?" I croaked.

"We've called for the doctor," she said in her best calming voice. "We just need to wait for him."

"What's going to happen?"

"I'm not sure. We just need to keep you still until the doc gets here."

"I'm getting really sore. Can someone get my legs onto the bed?"

"Not yet. We don't want to move you until we talk to the doc. Try to stay still."

Sure, no problem. Just stay still, as though I could move even if I wanted to. "What's going to happen? Am I all right?"

"You're going to be fine," she replied in the calm-nurse voice. "Try to stay still and quiet."

The fake-calm act wasn't convincing me.

After a while, Julie returned and stood beside me. I could tell she'd been crying. "I'm so sorry, Rich," she whispered. "How are you?"

I lied. "I'm OK. Any sign of the doc yet?"

"His nurse just called. He's in surgery right now. One of the nurses went to tell him what happened and see what we can do. She should be back soon."

My body still twisted awkwardly, legs hanging heavily to my right. The rigid halo jacket was cumbersome and constricting anyway, but now it dug painfully into my back and side. "Can you move my legs? This is really uncomfortable."

"That's one of the questions she'll ask. Hang in there. We'll have an answer soon." Then she leaned over and touched my arm. "Rich, I'm so sorry."

"Don't worry. It'll be fine." I wished I really believed that.

Julie and Eleanor talked for a moment. Eleanor and I were apparently going to be attached for a while, and her improvised position forced her to lean awkwardly. Julie got a chair and they tried to arrange a better posture, then she left to check for news from the surgeon.

It seemed like hours, but it was probably just a few minutes before she returned. "News from the doctor," she reported. "Sorry it took so long, but he's in the middle of a back surgery, and he's the only neurosurgeon on call today. He took a quick break to talk to us." Apparently she had gotten impatient and gone downstairs as well. "He said he wasn't too concerned about any further damage because the fusion should be pretty solid by now." Well, sounds good so far.

"Did you ask about moving my legs?"

"Yes. He said we could make you more comfortable as long as we keep your neck as still as possible. So I've got some help coming and we'll get you situated." Soon several assistants arrived. Someone helped hold my head, and my legs were finally lifted onto the bed. I was still twisted sort of sideways, but at least the hard jacket wasn't stabbing me in the ribs, and I could relax while we awaited the next move. They raised the protective rails on the hospital bed, and Eleanor was able to adjust her stance and relax a bit.

"Now what?" I asked.

"Well, he needs to finish the surgery first. He told us he would get in touch with Dr. Warson to figure out what to do next, so now we just need to wait."

The panic subsided a bit. Maybe this wouldn't be a big deal after all. Another question. "Will they have to re-attach the thing?"

"Not sure. That's part of what he wants to discuss with Dr. Warson. We just have to wait to see what they decide."

Maybe this would be a blessing in disguise. If the fusion had healed, maybe I'd get rid of the halo a few weeks early. THAT would be something to celebrate with my dad.

So we waited—and waited—and waited. I guess whoever was having back surgery had first claim on his surgeon. Go figure. Lunch arrived, but I couldn't eat in this odd position. Eleanor still cradled my head and shoulders, and we waited. Julie came back into the room.

"He just called. He's out of surgery and he talked to Dr. Warson. He'll be here in a few minutes."

"So what's going to happen?" I asked. I just wanted to change positions again. I'd been thinking about my dad's visit and hoped I could get out of bed and work on extending my sitting time. I hadn't really considered what "re-attaching" the halo might involve.

But there was that expression again, the one that said she really didn't want to tell me something. "So what does that mean? Can I get rid of the halo? How do they put it back? Will I have another surgery?" Rapid-fire questions once more, and she couldn't, or didn't want to, provide answers. Perhaps this wasn't going to be so simple after all. I'd learned there is no "minor surgery." Anesthesia, recovery and Intensive Care are never "minor," especially when someone's going to drill holes in your skull. Was I about to lose all of the ground I'd gained?

"Let's wait until he gets here," she repeated, but this obviously wasn't a small issue. I could see tears welling up in her eyes again. She turned and left the room. What was going on?

I asked Eleanor if she knew what was happening. I still couldn't see her face, but the calm-nurse voice betrayed her concern as she told me to just try to relax and wait for the doctor.

Anyone who's been in a hospital knows "the doctor will be here in a few minutes" really means "you'll see the doctor sometime, but don't hold your breath." So we waited, and that just gave me more time to wonder about whatever Julie didn't want to tell me. I'd become really good at imagining the worst possible outcome. This was a situation ideally suited to that particular skill, and I became progressively more agitated. By the time he finally arrived in the middle of the afternoon, I could scarcely breathe from fear of the imaginary scenarios I'd created.

Neurosurgeons aren't known for their sensitive bedside manner, and this guy fit the stereotype. He took a quick look at the situation and issued some brief orders. Almost as an afterthought, he spoke to me.

"Dr. Warson and I talked it over, and we're going to re-attach your halo." He reported this with the sensitivity of an auto mechanic telling me my car needed a new fuel pump.

"So, where does that happen?" I whispered. "Do you take me to an operating room?"

"We don't want to risk moving you that much," he replied. "We'll do it right here."

Panic tightened around my chest and I tried unsuccessfully to slow my breathing and relax. They'd originally screwed the thing to my head during surgery. How could they do it here in a regular hospital room? "Do we use some kind of local anesthetic?"

"No, we can't do that here. They're getting some stuff from downstairs right now. I'll be back in a few minutes." And with that bit of encouragement, he turned and walked out the door.

The reality of what he said began to sink in and I felt a wave of terror that seemed to squeeze the breath from my lungs. In a few minutes he intended to come through that door and put screws in my head, and I would be awake while it happened! Now I understood what Julie didn't want to tell me.

I thought I'd experienced fear during the past weeks, but this was terror at an entirely new level. How do you just lie still while a guy puts screws in your skull? Eleanor tried to reassure me, but the calm-nurse bit did little to relieve the dread that seemed to strangle me. Julie reappeared, her eyes red, looking about as scared as I felt. She tried the cheery act, but she wasn't fooling either of us. "Rich," she finally murmured, "I'm so sorry. What can I do for you?"

"Did they tell you what's going to happen?"

"Yes. The equipment from the O.R. just arrived. He should be back in just a moment. I'll be right here."

"How can they do this? How can they put screws in my head and think I can just lie here calmly while they do it?" I could barely speak at all, and I'm certain even my hoarse croak of a voice communicated the desperate horror churning inside me. There must be another way, something that can get me out from this. This can't be real! Even the most sadistic screenwriter wouldn't imagine a scene so macabre.

Julie didn't know what to say. She felt guilty, as though this was her fault. It wasn't. She hadn't done anything wrong at all. I wanted to reassure her, but I was so terrified at the thought of what was about to happen that I couldn't find the words. I wanted to know exactly what to expect. "How far into my skull do the screws have to go?"

She held up a plastic bag. Inside were four small rods; they looked like little fine-threaded machine screws, except that the ends weren't sharply pointed. She spoke softly. "They don't really screw into the skull. They just press tightly against your head directly opposite each other."

Oh, that's all? No problem. Can't even imagine why I was worried. Instead of putting holes in my head, he's just going to smash it. Glad that's cleared up.

"Do you know how much it'll hurt?"

She shook her head slowly. "He ordered a topical anesthetic to deaden the skin, but I really don't know how much you'll feel." She sounded as frightened as I was. "I'll be right here with you." I appreciated that, but I was still scared to death.

This time the doctor told the truth when he said he'd be back in a few minutes. He bustled into the room, inspected the equipment from the OR, and began barking orders. Three or four other people entered the room and positioned themselves around my bed, ready to hold me still as this torture began. The doc hardly acknowledged my presence; I guess his patients were usually asleep while he worked on them.

Some shots into my scalp and forehead—I guess that's the topical anesthetic. *Ouch, that stings!* My arms and legs were pinned by all of the surrounding hands, but I could feel Julie holding my right hand between her own. She squeezed as I winced from the pain of the shots.

Now he held a screwdriver—maybe that's why he talked like an auto mechanic. He opened the plastic hardware bag; I could feel him jerk and pull the halo up and into position. There's the first screw; I felt it press against my forehead. Well, that wasn't so bad. Maybe this really won't be such a big deal. Now the second screw, against the back of my head, opposite the first one.

Oh my gosh! He cranked on the screwdriver, and I was certain my skull would collapse. I tried to yell; not much effect with my whisper of a voice. I strained against the hands clasped tightly on every part of my body and tried to focus on Julie's fingers squeezing my right hand. Now he worked on the third screw, and this time I knew what to expect. I attempted to brace myself, but preparing for the crushing pain was futile.

He worked quickly. Now the fourth screw pressed against my throbbing skull. My head felt like the jaws of a vise squeezed tighter and tighter until my cranium seemed certain to implode.

Thankfully, the entire procedure couldn't have taken more than a couple of minutes. The hands relaxed their grip and Eleanor could finally stop cradling my neck and shoulders. She held me still for—how long? Maybe three hours? She walked beside my bed, stretching her neck and shoulders. She smiled, patted my shoulder and walked from the room without a word. The doctor had disappeared, promising to return in a couple of hours to check on me. Great—can't wait for that visit.

Julie and I sat in the now-deserted room. She still clutched my hand almost desperately. "Rich—are you all right?"

"Yeah," I croaked. "But my head really hurts."

"The doc said it might be pretty sore for a while. He left a prescription for the pain. How about if I get it for you?"

"Thanks. That would be good." She squeezed my hand again then hustled out the door, relieved to finally be able to do something to help.

I was alone in my home-away-from-home. I took a deep breath and exhaled slowly, trying to remove my focus from the squeezing, pounding pain of the four screws pressing against my head. Julie returned with some pills and found me crying. "Oh, Rich," she whispered. "Is it bad?"

"How can this be happening to me? What am I going to do?" I sobbed. She held my hand again, unable to summon the comforting words she sought. She helped me swallow the pain pills then sat beside me on the mattress.

After a while she spoke quietly. "Did the doc tell you when he was coming back?"

"Not really. He just said he'd be back in a couple of hours to check on me. Maybe he just wants to sit and chat." My feeble attempt at humor didn't elicit much of a laugh. She smiled weakly then glanced at the floor. I spotted that look again. She tried to conceal her concern.

"What?" Panic rose once more in my throat. "What's wrong? What did he say?" She looked at me sadly, her eyes becoming misty once more.

"He said he has to . . ." She hesitated, choking a bit on her words. "He has to tighten the screws to make sure they don't break loose again."

Tighten the screws? He's going to crank on them again? Fear knotted my stomach, and I thought I might vomit. My head threatened to cave in, and he's going to *tighten the screws more*?

That's not possible. She must have misunderstood. Maybe he was making a little doctor joke and she didn't get it. No way this can be real. Terror simply wouldn't allow me to believe such a thing was possible.

Julie saw the fear and the questions racing through my smashed head. "He said he has to make sure the screws are tight enough to keep the halo in place. We sure don't want this to happen again." My head pounded; how could my skull possibly absorb any more pressure without collapsing? How could the screws conceivably need to be tighter?

So I waited. He said he'd be back around 5:00 P.M., which of course really meant he might appear sometime before morning. Waiting for the initial procedure had been difficult, not sure what to expect, and imagining all of the worst possibilities. But now I *knew* what would happen. My head felt mashed like an old rotten Halloween pumpkin, and he planned to increase the pressure on pins that already felt like they protruded into my brain.

Nothing relieved the terror of anticipation. I tried to watch TV to divert my thoughts from the fear. I cringed every time I heard footsteps in the hallway, wanting to finally get it done and over, but hoping it wasn't him. Dinner arrived, but I couldn't imagine eating. Minutes crawled by until another hour passed, then two. Julie came in a few times, apologetic; nothing from the doc yet, we'll let you know as soon as we hear something.

The nursing shift changed at 7:00, but Julie stayed even though she'd been here for more than twelve hours. This had been an exhausting ordeal for her, but she wasn't going anywhere until the surgeon completed the final stage of the torture. She kept apologizing, and I tried to reassure her that it wasn't her fault. Right now, only an end to the torment would make anything better.

So we waited.

Finally, at about 7:30 he arrived, bursting into the room with several people in tow. He carried a small metal toolbox, as if he was going to repair the pipes or operate on the heater. Once more everyone gathered around my bed, ready to hold me still. Julie clutched my hand again, but my attention focused on the toolbox.

He opened the lid, reached inside, and pulled out a torque wrench! I stared in disbelief. He approached me with the same tool you use to tighten the dead bolts on a car engine. This special device includes a little gauge allowing bolts to be screwed onto specs, tight enough without over-doing it and damaging something. I didn't know whether to scream in fear or laugh at the preposterous notion that he intended to perform a medical procedure with a common mechanic's tool. The only missing items were greasy hands and the mechanic's uniform with his name above the pocket.

He must have seen the incredulous look on my face, because finally he actually spoke to me. "This will just take a minute," he said matter-of-factly. "We just have to make sure the screws are tightened correctly."

Great, I thought. Maybe you can change the oil and rotate the tires while you're here.

Hands grasped me once again; I squeezed my eyes shut, clenched my teeth and waited for the wrench to grasp the first pin.

It wasn't quite as bad as I'd expected. My head already hurt so much that I guess it couldn't get much worse, and maybe the pain pills I'd taken earlier helped a little. I was certain that he cranked the screws through my skull and into my brain. The intense pressure was excruciating, but the pain didn't get much worse. He worked quickly, cranking all four screws to the correct amount of force in a couple of minutes.

"There, all done. Dr. Warson will be in to check on you in the morning." He tossed the wrench back in the toolbox, closed the latch and breezed out the door.

"I wonder if I have to come in for a three thousand mile check-up," I joked half-heartedly. The nurses and aides standing around my bed laughed nervously, then they also hustled out of the room. Julie still had my hand in a death grip.

She looked up slowly. "Are you OK?"

"Yeah. That really wasn't as bad as I expected. I just never expected a brain surgeon to come after me with a set of Craftsman tools."

She giggled a little. "Can I do anything for you before I leave?"

"No, go home," I replied. "I think I just need some rest right now. You too—you look exhausted. It's been a long day, huh?"

Her face strained with emotion and stress, and she looked like she could collapse at any moment. She started to apologize again, but I stopped her. "Listen to me. You didn't do anything wrong. This wasn't your fault. Stop beating yourself up."

I could see that she didn't really believe me, but she released her grip on my hand and stood beside my bed. Tears misted in her eyes again. "Are you working tomorrow?" I asked.

"Yeah, bright and early." She half-smiled. She was trying to get back to being cheery-nurse, but the stress of the day collapsed the facade. "I'll see you in the morning."

"Get some rest. And remember what I said—this wasn't your fault." She smiled weakly, touched my arm, and trudged slowly out the door.

I lay there quietly, listening to the familiar, muffled evening hospital sounds. My head still felt like it was crushed in a vise, but the pain was a bit less intense. I was really tired, and I worried about Julie. I heard her say "Good night" and then heard the hallway door open and close. I suspected she would have a difficult night. No matter what I said, she was still going to blame herself for this awful incident that wasn't anybody's fault. I was glad she worked in the morning. Even though the night would be short and she'd be tired, at least I could see her and reassure her.

I fumbled with the remote and flipped on the television to take my mind off the pain. In a little while one of the night nurses came in with my evening drugs. I took more pain pills and something to help me sleep, and the routine of the hospital slowly returned and displaced tension and fear. I was beyond tired, no doubt due to some combination of drugs and the fading adrenaline rush.

Before sleep came, I thought a little about my dad's visit, now only one day away. I wondered if I would still be able to sit up, whether this painful vice grip sensation would subside, and what all of this would do to him. What would he see when he was confronted by the monster in the mirror?

Julie awakened me for breakfast. Usually the morning sounds as the hospital got up and running for the day made sleeping past 6:00 A.M. impossible, but the drugs I'd received during the night apparently allowed me to ignore the noise for an extra hour of badly needed slumber. Her eyes betrayed weariness, but she at least pretended to be her usual cheerful self. "So, how are you this morning?" she asked in that familiar, upbeat voice.

"Well, I'm still asleep," I muttered. She pulled back the blinds and sunlight streamed into the room. I squinted in the sudden bright light. "At least, I was asleep until you showed up."

"Time to get up and get going. Breakfast is here and you need to get ready for therapy." Then she stopped bustling around the room, dropped the cheery act for a moment, and asked quietly, "How is your head?"

"Hurts," I whispered. "But not like last night. Mostly it just feels like my hat's way too tight. It'd be even better if *someone* wasn't trying to blind me so early in the morning," I teased. Then a bit more seriously, "Really, it's not so bad. Don't worry."

"Thanks." Julie smiled weakly. She looked like she needed a long nap, and she faced a twelve-hour shift. But she resumed her nursing activities, getting clothes and shoes from the closet to help me get dressed. Over her shoulder she asked, "By the way, isn't your dad coming tomorrow?"

"Yeah." I realized how weary I felt. "What if I skip therapy this morning?"

She stopped and turned around. "Are you sure? The staff talked about it when I got here this morning, but it might be good to get up and move around a little."

I didn't understand at the time, but I'd arrived at another of those seemingly insignificant moments that ultimately determined the nature of my path. I'd worked toward a goal, accomplished small-but-important gains, and actually focused on someone other than myself. Almost by accident, I moved in a positive direction. I could have worked past the headache, gone to therapy, joked about having screws in my brain, and made this a positive day. The broken halo would have generated some good hospital humor with the physical therapists. I'll never know what might have happened if I had heeded Julie's advice.

I'll never know, because in that moment, I chose to fall back into the quagmire of self-pity and hopelessness. Rather than choosing to demonstrate to myself that I could overcome the unfortunate setback of the previous day, I decided to go back to the familiar give-up, no-hope approach that doomed me to make so little progress since my injury. Rather than moving forward, I used the pain as an excuse to return to working only at convincing those around me that my life was useless and the best they could do was feel sorry for me.

I chose to skip therapy that morning. Julie knew it was pointless to try and change my mind. So I took more drugs, stayed in bed, watched television, and postponed once again the inevitable day when I would finally face the reality of my injury, take stock of all that remained, and get on with living my life.

My dad and step-mom arrived the next day. I sensed Dad's nervous energy. I did manage to sit up for much of their brief visit, but between the pain meds and my newly reborn sense of hopelessness, I don't think I painted the positive picture I'd hoped. My head still hurt, conversations were strained, and I demonstrated only that things were not going very well. Somehow I'd wanted to I could spare them from the reality of my lack of progress.

After dinner I was back in bed, the transfer done especially carefully, and they prepared to leave. I could see the strain of this day on their faces, but I didn't know what to do to make it better. As they were about to go, Dad turned to me and, almost pleading, asked, "Is there anything I can do for you?" My dad is a man of action, worked hard all of his life; he wanted more than anything to be able to do something about this horrible situation that made him feel so helpless. I could see it in his eyes—*just tell me what I can do to help.*

I had no idea what to say because I had no hope that anything anyone did could free me from this useless body and broken life. I nearly replied, *No, Dad, there isn't anything anyone can do.* But from nowhere a random thought popped into my head.

"A Heath Bar," I croaked.

"What?" He wasn't accustomed to my weak, whispery voice.

"A Heath Bar sounds really good."

"A Heath Bar—you mean the candy bar?"

"Yeah. For some reason that sounds really good."

"OK," he said, and nearly ran out of the door, Marje scrambling to catch up.

I laughed to myself. Heath Bar? I couldn't recall the last time I ate one of them. Where did I come up with that idea?

Rules on the rehab unit were less strict than the rest of the hospital, but formal visiting hours ended long ago. I figured I'd see Dad in the morning. The nurse brought my bedtime meds and helped me get undressed. I settled down for the night.

A quiet light from the nighttime hallway outlined Dad's form as he burst abruptly through the door with Marje still trying to keep pace. He carried a large brown grocery bag.

"Here you are," he announced. "Heath Bars. Sorry we took so long."

I leaned over the edge of my bed and peered into the bag—dozens of Heath Bars! "You must have bought every one in the store."

"Actually, several stores." Marje chuckled. "Your dad wanted to make sure you had enough."

"Yeah, the first couple of places didn't have many," he said. "You'd think people in this town never heard of Heath Bars. Here, do you want one?"

No way I could open the wrapper with my crippled hands, so he ripped it open and handed it to me. I crunched into the chocolate and toffee, savoring the tastes and textures as the candy quickly disappeared.

"Want another one?" He started to tear another wrapper open. I laughed.

"No, Dad, one's enough for tonight. But thanks. That really hit the spot."

He pulled open the drawer on the bedside table and dumped the bag. "OK, I'll put them in here where you can reach them if you want." Heath Bars stuffed the drawer. "I'll put the rest in the closet. You can ask somebody to reach them if you need more."

"Good." I chuckled. "If I eat more than a few dozen, I'll know where to find more."

"Smartass," he shot back with a grin. "I could just take them all with me."

"No!" I said in feigned panic. "They're good right where they are."

"Well, all right. We'll go then and let you get some rest."

Marje said, "Goodbye," and they turned to go. Then Dad stopped and walked back to my bed. He looked down at me.

"Fight hard," he said quietly.

After they left, I craved another candy bar. I'd never even tried to retrieve anything from that drawer, and I started to reach for the call button to ask for help. Then I hesitated and decided to see if I could do it by myself. I fumbled for a time, but managed to hook a finger on the drawer handle. I pulled and the drawer slid open, revealing my enticing stash of candy.

I dipped my hand into the pile, and after a lot of experimenting, managed to snag one and pull it onto the bed. The wrapper eventually yielded to a messy combination of fingers and teeth and I enjoyed my first independent snack. The candy tasted delightful; I only wish I had relished the satisfaction of the considerable step forward it represented.

I didn't give up. I didn't ask for help. I wanted a candy bar, and I figured out how to get it. It wasn't easy or smooth, but if I'd thought about it, I might have realized that I wasn't completely helpless. Another important lesson missed.

I had plenty of Heath Bars for myself and for all of the nurses and therapists who shared them. The headache subsided in a few days, and soon the only reminder of that difficult day was a slightly askew view of the world. Apparently the doctor/mechanic didn't quite get the halo into just the perfect position in our improvised surgical environment, so the brace now held my head firmly but just barely turned to the right. For the next six weeks, I had to look a bit sideways at everything.

Well, there was one other reminder of that "memorable" Valentine's Day. I would now have four scars on my forehead by which to remember the brace and that horrible, frightening day.

IS THIS WHO I THINK IT IS?

Most of my hospital experience had thankfully faded into the background. I didn't expect this innocent communication to dredge up so many difficult recollections.

Too bad I didn't know where she was on her birthday. I could have given her a candy bar!

As these seven words prompted me to sift through the events that comprised the entire experience of my injury, I wondered which were crucial to the outcome? Which moments shaped the totality of that horrible time? What seemingly insignificant interactions ultimately determined how this tragedy would be resolved? Which scenes enhance the play's plot? Which characters would the audience want to meet?

CHAPTER 9

ELEVATOR

Weekends on the rehab unit entailed a unique brand of self-imposed loneliness. Minimal staffing forced cancellation of regular physical and occupational therapy sessions. Other patients spent time with family or friends, but I rejected nearly all visitors so my days were mostly quiet and solitary.

The staff usually rented movies, if you didn't mind sitting in the lounge with other patients and guests who wanted to be there as little as you did. Nurses and aides offered games that would have provided great therapy for my slowly improving hands and arms, but I became embarrassed and frustrated when I fumbled cards and dropped game pieces. Instead of persisting, I usually gave up and retreated in anger to the isolation of my room.

Weekends permitted time to achieve independent goals such as extending my tolerance for sitting in the chair. The broken halo experience became my excuse to regress into despair and hopelessness. My defeatist attitude significantly slowed this initial step in my recovery, but finally I developed the endurance to sit an hour or more in relative comfort.

My next wheelchair goal seems remarkably trivial in retrospect. After I could sit safely, the therapists established a new target: they challenged me to push my chair ten feet without stopping.

Ten feet! Mark off ten feet on the floor. You can probably *jump* ten feet! Despite the demands posed by the heavy, bulky chair, it's still difficult to believe that I struggled to move such a short distance.

I wasted weeks not accomplishing this goal. Even though I only gave it minimal effort, it was still only ten feet. How hard could it be? Each session required a nurse to push me into the hallway, because I couldn't overcome the carpeted rehab unit floors. The shiny, waxed tiles marked one-foot squares, so I'd count out ten of them, make a mental note of where I was headed, and off I'd go. Time and time again I'd roll two or three feet and stop. I just couldn't do it. One-third of a football first down always required three or four attempts.

I weighed about one hundred eighty five pounds when I fell. Inactivity and the bout of pneumonia caused my weight to plummet more than forty-five pounds in the weeks following the accident. My arms resembled sticks, and the clumsy, heavy halo brace restricted my movements and made me top-heavy. Combining these real obstacles with my lack of effort, ten feet might as well have been ten miles.

Doctors, nurses, and therapists tried to help me regain badly needed strength. They designed special weight-lifting routines to accommodate my lack of mobility, but I put more effort into complaining about discomfort and difficulty than into actually doing the work. If I had directed my anger at the weights, I would have made a lot of progress.

Additional food appeared on my tray for each meal. A can of liquid supplement frequently remained opened but untouched on my bedside tray. Almost every day, when I returned from therapy in the afternoon, I was greeted by a cheeseburger and a chocolate milkshake. Any concerted effort at my prescribed exercises would have converted those calories into muscle and made quick work of the ten-foot goal.

Instead, I drank the milkshakes (I hadn't totally lost my mind!), picked at the burgers, largely ignored the supplements, and exercised half-heartedly at best. I didn't gain the strength I needed, and those miserable ten feet remained a seemingly insurmountable obstacle.

ELEVATOR

Day after day I struggled and failed. I'd use any available excuse to avoid the work. When nobody was watching, I'd just sit and stare out the window or pretend to contemplate the artwork. I groaned and moaned and grunted and strained and made a great show of trying hard, but each time my arms began to tire, I stopped. Ten feet was too far! The therapists encouraged, cajoled, laughed, and became irritated and impatient, but they couldn't force me to push through my discomfort and lack of faith.

During the week, therapy appointments, doctor visits, and a myriad of real and imagined tasks diverted attention from the ten-foot goal. I claimed exhaustion from the therapy sessions, obviously an excuse rather than a reason, since the therapists did most of the work. I invented creative schemes to avoid the effort required to overcome that terrible ten-foot hurdle.

These flimsy attempts at rationalization evaporated on weekends. On Saturdays and Sundays I was alone with just my stick-man arms, the huge, heavy chair, and those ten one-foot tile squares.

I worked harder at justifying my lack of achievement than at surmounting this important obstacle, and excuses abounded. The halo brace locked my upper body in a rigid, upright position. Since no muscles functioned in my back or abdomen, any quick movement threatened to destroy my precarious balance and send me toppling forward to the floor. The back of the chair reclined to provide stability, creating an awkward position from which to push the wheels. I became quite accomplished at being pathetic, so it was difficult for family, friends, and hospital folks to encourage, much less demand, the kind of effort required to move the chair more than a foot or two.

Footrests angled forward from the front of the chair to assist in the reclining motion. Because the reclining posture shifted the center of gravity and might cause the chair to tip backwards, the wheels were positioned too far back for efficient use. The chair weighed nearly sixty pounds—three or four times the weight of a normal wheelchair.

The awkward design did not promote easy or efficient movement, and I reminded everyone of that fact continuously. How could they expect me to propel this unwieldy overweight contraption? I complained constantly, and wasn't beyond trying to induce a bit of guilt from anyone who questioned my lack of commitment. "You try it," I'd croak. "You get a halo screwed to your head, sit in this monster chair in this awkward position, and see how hard it really is!"

Even for those who realized I was just making excuses to avoid taking responsibility for my own recovery, this pathetic act was difficult to overcome. The facts were clear: it *was* unfair and it *was* incredibly difficult. Others could not possibly put themselves in my place or imagine my experience. And one other fact became painfully clear. No one could force me do the work or make the effort for me. Nobody else can unlock your personal prison cell. Until I decided to move forward, I couldn't move forward. That's just the way it was, and I knew it. I didn't like it, and I refused to accept it.

One Sunday I set off to not-work on the ten feet. This simple beginning goal had become an impediment to the rest of my rehab. A lot of other important steps such as learning independent transfers, getting fitted for a lighter, more efficient chair, and any sort of independent strength training couldn't even begin until I could move around at least a little bit by myself. So I struggled a few feet at a time down the hall, around a corner, and out of sight.

I was becoming pretty familiar with the layout of the hospital. On the few occasions when I allowed visitors to see me, we usually went on "walks" to get away from the cramped room on the rehab unit. This mostly meant I pushed the chair a short distance, complained a lot, and convinced my companion to push the chair so we could get somewhere.

On this Sunday, I discovered a door propped open that led into the education area of the hospital. I moved slowly past the medical library and a couple of classrooms. The carpeting in the halls normally would have defeated me, but I pressed forward, not really aware of how far I was going. I was happy to be away from the watchful eyes of the rehab staff.

ELEVATOR

This area was nearly deserted. A few people worked in the library, but I crept along past some seldom-used elevators with a destination now in mind.

I rounded another corner and saw a small seating area next to a window. I'd been here before and knew that from this window I could look out on a small rose garden. I hadn't ventured outside of the hospital since the accident, and I wanted just to look at the world beyond the window. I could sit here, rest a few minutes, and watch the traffic move past the hospital before I began my return journey. This vacant alcove provided a peaceful respite from the smells, sounds, and sterility of the hospital.

Someone had left two chairs right in front of the window. Anyone else would have simply rearranged the furniture, but with my stick-arms, heavy chair, and lack of initiative, this obstacle thwarted my plan to enjoy even one small moment of peace. I couldn't possibly move those chairs, because you certainly can't succeed at a task you won't even attempt.

So I just stared out the window at the gray January sky. Clouds moved slowly past my little portal to the outside. Perfect for my circumstances, I thought, overcast and dreary, like the sky I saw in the background when I looked up at that paramedic several weeks ago.

My daydream was interrupted. The speaker above my head sounded, "Rich Dixon, please return to your room." What do they want?

I was in no rush to return. For once I focused on something other than my misery. I'd discovered a calm oasis in the storm that had surrounded me, a peaceful place to pass the hours of another endless Sunday. My prison cell of a room offered nothing but more mind-numbing TV. The quiet solitude here was comforting. Why couldn't they just leave me alone for a few peaceful minutes?

I heard my name over the speaker a few more times, disrupting even this brief moment of serenity. I struggled to turn the chair on the carpet, noticed a clock, and realized I'd been gone for several hours. This small nook was quite a long distance from "home," and I'd been in the chair much longer than usual. The return trip promised to be difficult.

I pushed just a few feet across the carpet when a hospital security guard appeared. "So, there you are." He grabbed his walkie-talkie, reported his discovery, and began to push my chair down the hallway. I didn't object, another apparently insignificant choice in a long sequence of missed opportunities.

Though I failed to understand at the time, I made important progress that day. I ventured on my own into strange territory for the first time since the accident and discovered a relatively tranquil spot in which to contemplate the awful turn my life had taken. No nurses or therapists looked after me, no hospital schedules told me when and where to go, no assistants helped when I got frustrated or tired.

Too bad that security guard located me so quickly. Had I made the demanding journey back to the rehab unit, I might have learned something from my unplanned excursion. I might have recognized some of the possibilities concealed within this new life and acknowledged I could overcome many of the limitations and barriers that initially seemed so insurmountable. I might have learned that serenity could be discovered even in the prison of this hospital. As it was, I'd wait a while to explore the confines of my broken life.

I don't remember the moment I actually surpassed the ten-foot barrier, but after my Sunday disappearance, I slowly began pushing the chair a bit more on my own. That spontaneous outing did have one tangible result; the rehab staff now concocted my next tortuous task and altered my familiar daily routine. The change led to one of the most discouraging and most humorous experiences of my incarceration in the hospital.

Under this latest arrangement, an aide would no longer fetch me prior to each therapy session; I had to get myself to the physical therapy clinic and back. This modification concealed a number of additional challenges. It not only involved the extra work of traveling to and from the clinic, but this journey of thirty minutes or more required me to leave earlier and return later for each appointment. Their new plan incorporated more work, more chair time, and less time in bed. I protested to no avail.

On the Saturday before implementation of the new strategy, the nurses decided I should attempt a trial run. I was now a veteran of the hospital corridors, so I guess they thought they could trust me out of their sight. Actually, I suspect that after enduring weeks of my whining, they were eager to get rid of me.

So off I went one fateful Saturday morning. The carpeted hallway of the rehab unit grabbed at my wheels like quicksand, and the automatic doors blocked my escape route. I pushed the button with the happy little wheelchair icon, moved with lighting speed toward the open door, then sagged in defeat as the door closed slowly while I remained several feet from freedom. I'd learned someone would eventually enter from the outside world, so I just waited in front of the door until it finally opened.

Once I conquered the doors, I rolled down the tile hallway that now required only a few stops to rest my aching shoulders as I dashed twenty-five or thirty feet at a time! Rounding the final corner, I encountered a previously unconsidered obstacle: the elevator.

A hospital elevator might appear easily accessible. Smooth floors, wide entrance, clearly labeled controls installed at the proper height. No sweat, right? Well, not quite.

I chose the staff elevators located a little farther from my room than the public elevators used by visitors. I wanted to avoid people as much as possible. Because it was Saturday, the staff elevators were less populated. In a few moments this would prove to be a mixed blessing.

I eased up to the call buttons and maneuvered until they waited directly in front of me at eye level. But with my halo brace and lack of stability I couldn't reach forward to press the button without falling on my nose. I needed another approach.

I backed up, which was much more difficult than going forward. I turned until I sat beside the buttons. I could just barely reach out to press one.

Uh-oh. Pushing the buttons required a new set of movements. My arms still lacked complete control, especially when I reached away from my body. I tried to brace against the armrest, reach out, and—my fingers didn't work. How do you push a button without using your fingers?

I could use my thumb a bit; so maybe my thumb could press the button. Braced again, I zeroed in on the "DOWN" arrow, and stabbed. A few misses, and then—SUCCESS! The button illuminated. I heard the elevator begin to move, responding to the call of my wavering arm and barely controlled thumb.

Two chimes signaled the elevator's arrival. Unfortunately, it wasn't the car in front of me. I heard the doors open behind me as I struggled to back up.

I didn't even get close. The elevator waited a few seconds, declared a false alarm, and moved on. I turned just enough to see the doors slide shut.

I rested a few minutes. Moving the chair quickly made my shoulders burn and arms ache. While I waited, the elevator returned, and a man in hospital scrubs emerged. Do you need a hand? Hold the door for you?

No. I didn't want him to watch me struggle to get turned and into the elevator. I flailed my arm to wave him on.

Ready for another attempt, I rolled beside the controls and stabbed at the button. My fumbling thumb hit the "UP" arrow. Oh, well. I decided to accept whatever showed up.

Quick! Back and turn. I heard the car moving. Back a little more, and I was in position directly in front of the doors. The bell chimed once, but the other set of doors opened! I hadn't considered that possibility.

ELEVATOR

I turned and pushed forward, but as the doors closed I sat several feet away.

I cursed in frustration. Why are these elevators so hard to use? Why don't they wait longer? I'll never get off this floor without help! This isn't fair!

I decided I would have to press the button, choose my door, and push toward it immediately. I moved too slowly to wait and see which car arrived.

I teach math. I've made up all sorts of silly probability questions using marbles, coins, dice, busses, and elevators. Who cares? Well, now I cared. Which one would arrive next? The score was two to one. I'd ask my students to calculate experimental probabilities and make a prediction based on a data table and a graph. Which one should I choose?

As I stabbed at the button again, I decided to bet on the car in front of me. Each elevator is equally likely to appear, and I could get there faster because I didn't have to back up.

The DOWN arrow lighted again. First try! I rolled forward, turned, and faced the doors. The signal sounded. I looked up and the other doors opened, waited those few miserable seconds, and closed.

With any thought at all, I should have just stayed where I was. Just like the automatic door on the rehab unit, someone eventually would have emerged from that car, and I'd have been ready to jump through the doors.

Unfortunately, stubbornness and frustration supplanted clear-headed reasoning and problem solving. So I struggled around in a half-circle and prepared for another try. But I faced the question again—which one should I choose? The score stood three to one for the choice on the right. Does that make the other more likely? Should I change my bet?

Nope. I decided to stick with my initial guess. I probably wouldn't reach the alternative anyway because of the backing-up thing. No, this had to be the winner this time. I was becoming a fairly proficient button-pusher. I pressed and scrambled to turn, the car arrived, and now the score became four to one. The doors opened and closed. They probably just appeared to smirk as they eased together.

Now what? What are the odds? As the wrong car appeared and departed once more, I slumped with defeat. If I hadn't been so angry and frustrated, I might have chuckled at the thought of students dutifully taking notes while I assured them that elevators don't know the odds and can't remember that the score is now five to one.

I wondered if mine was broken, but it did come that one time. Yeah, but maybe it broke right after that. Maybe somebody stopped it on another floor.

I wasn't changing, committed now as a matter of either principle or stubbornness. Besides, I would really feel stupid if I switched and my original choice appeared.

Turn, stab, light, scramble. I heard the whir of machinery, but which one would appear? I stared at the lights, expecting another failure.

A double chime signaled an arrival and a victorious adrenaline rush accompanied the parting of the shiny silver doors before me. I couldn't stop to rejoice. I rolled forward, prepared to celebrate my triumphant passage through the winning portal.

Instead, I encountered once more a basic principle of my recovery process: no important gain would ever happen easily.

People walk on and off elevators without even noticing the tiny crack between the floor and the car, but my attention now focused intently on that insignificant crevice that suddenly swallowed the front wheels of my chair. Conquest instantly reverted to defeat as I sat trapped in the doorway.

The automatic doors began to close. A sensor responded to my presence and halted the motion. After a few seconds the mechanism made another attempt. Over and over, the doors would close a bit and then part once more.

I was stuck. Stuck in the elevator doorway, in the bulky chair, in the hospital, in my miserable broken body. Stuck and trapped, a perfect metaphor for what remained of what was once my life.

I've since learned to overcome much more significant obstacles, and with the lightweight chair I now use, I can easily jump my wheels over such small gaps. But I'd scarcely learned to make minimal progress on smooth, level floors, and I had no inkling how to escape from this unanticipated ambush. The doors continued to open, try to close, then stop and open again.

I honestly do not know how I finally managed to become unstuck. I tried forward, backward, and eventually, I somehow managed to free my wheels from their snare and rolled into the elevator.

I did it. Success! I'd entered the elevator completely by myself. It wasn't smooth, it wasn't easy, and it certainly wasn't efficient. But I'd overcome a significant challenge without help.

I then encountered another truth about my rehab that I would re-discover repeatedly over the next months. A triumph always fostered other, more difficult challenges. In a frustrating but seemingly inevitable cycle, the celebration of an advance inevitably preceded the frustration of a corresponding retreat.

Eventually I learned that I usually moved a bit farther forward than back, so continuous effort created slow but unmistakable progress. But it took a long time to discern this interplay of gain and loss and to develop the patience to accept this nearly imperceptible advancement as my new version of "normal."

As I rolled into the elevator I faced a serious tactical dilemma. The controls were right there, behind me, over my left shoulder, but I couldn't reach them. I needed to turn and get beside them as I had the call button.

Before I could solve this newest problem the doors closed and the car began moving. Well, that wasn't so bad. After all, I couldn't get lost. Up or down were my only options, and there were just five floors plus the basement where the clinic was located. I figured I would just push to the back of the car, make sure I was out of the way, and spin around.

I was going somewhere all on my own! Nobody lifted or pushed or helped, and until you're unable to move yourself you cannot appreciate the sense of freedom that accompanies independent motion.

I rolled slowly to the back of the car and began to turn. The advance/retreat principle of rehab appeared once more as I discovered I couldn't turn around within the confines of the elevator! The big clunky chair was too long, and the back hit one wall while the footrests banged against the other. I was stuck. Again.

I remember just wanting to quit right there, just stop and give up. All I'd overcome that day—carpet, automatic doors, long corridors, pushing buttons, picking the winning door, somehow escaping that crack. So many obstacles surmounted, and what had I accomplished? I was stuck in an elevator, facing the back wall and unable to move, dead-dog tired and discouraged. I imagined that this frustrating day represented a microcosm of the rest of my life. I would never be able to do anything. The entire process was hopeless.

Down and up, then the doors opened and someone boarded. We moved again, stopped, and the doors opened. People entered and departed behind me. I tried to ask for help, but the noise of machinery drowned my hoarse whisper of a voice. Life continued behind me while I remained jammed between the walls, locked rigid by the halo. I couldn't turn or talk. I could only stare at the blank rear wall.

I wish I could relate a courageous conclusion to a tale linking frustration and accomplishment. I'd like to report a clever escape from my predicament and a triumphant return to the rehab unit as conquering champion of the elevator. I'd like to claim some sort of inspirational moment of enlightenment when I suddenly realized I could achieve anything to which I set my mind. But that's not what happened.

Once again, I failed to discover lessons embedded within this discouraging incident. I just stared at the back of the elevator, convinced I was destined for a life filled with struggle and failure. I suppose I knew a staff member would eventually rescue me, though at the time I envisioned someone discovering my body days later, still riding up and down those six floors.

Finally, a concerned passenger decided to check on me. He leaned over my shoulder and asked if I was OK. I tried to shake my head but the halo held it steady, so I just croaked a quiet, "No." He helped me get back to the right floor and off the elevator. I rolled out into the hallway and paused for a long time, looking out a window. I could see the doctors' parking lot and the street beyond. People walked along on the sidewalk, doctors rushed in and out of their special entrance, cars came and went as the traffic light demanded.

Didn't they know life had ended? Didn't they know the world had been filled with pain and frustration and loss? How could they just keep on as if nothing had happened?

This movie hadn't ended. It wasn't time yet for the popcorn to be finished, for the final credits to roll. Happily-ever-after wasn't going to be the end of this show. How could all those people just pretend that the world was just as they left it, that the theater lights would come up and we'd all go back to some sort of existence that actually meant something?

DIDN'T THEY KNOW?

I struggled back to my room that day convinced I'd never make it, angry with everyone for making me try. I wanted more than anything to just be left alone!

Of course, I eventually conquered the elevator and other more difficult and fearsome obstacles. Thank God they didn't just leave me alone; despite my anger and disbelief, they kept me going.

When I'm at the hospital, I often ride that same elevator. I laugh when I recall guessing which car would arrive next and riding up and down, convinced my skeleton would be discovered after years of staring at the back of that stupid elevator.

I tell this story frequently, and I honestly think it's pretty funny to remember. The account always elicits a good laugh from listeners.

Of course, I don't include the part about the window and the cars and all of those who went on their way, oblivious to the fact that the world had ended.

That part wasn't so funny.

IS THIS WHO I THINK IT IS?

What was she doing when my world ended? How could I ever explain all of this—the despair, the humor, and the slow, nearly imperceptible progress? What would she think about the lack of effort?

Would she even want to know the details?

Would she want to meet the people who kept me going, who wouldn't take "I quit" for an answer?

CHAPTER 10

LEONARD

I met Leonard several months after my accident. I'd been discharged from the hospital following five months of incarceration disguised as in-patient rehab. As I began outpatient rehabilitation, I continued to work hard at not working.

Each day I arrived at the hospital for a session of physical therapy, a period of independent exercise, and some occupational therapy. Then I'd eat lunch and do more P.T. before going home. I remained feebly weak and had developed few essential wheelchair skills, so I badly needed the therapy and exercise. I needed to practice transferring to and from the chair, getting dressed, and using the bathroom safely and independently (think about *that* training for a moment). More importantly, this daily schedule forced me into public areas. I gradually learned to accomplish some tasks independently, such as using the cafeteria, but within the controlled and familiar hospital environment.

Regrettably, I steadfastly avoided most of the effort required to benefit from my new routine. I complained about pain, muscle spasms, exhaustion, heat, cold, and anything else I could invent. I was supposed to spend an hour each day pushing my chair around the quiet neighborhoods near the hospital. Designed to build strength and endurance, these "workouts" frequently consisted of sitting in one place for several minutes, rolling a few feet, and then stopping again. I didn't improve significantly, because I just couldn't summon the hope required to overcome pain and discomfort.

I'd finally graduated from the clumsy, heavy reclining wheelchair to a lighter everyday model. I could have made significant gains, but the solution involved more than equipment. A company called Sportaid uses a great slogan: *It's not what you push; it's what pushes you.* I could make no meaningful advancement until I could find something inside myself to push me. Though I could no longer blame the bulky chair or the halo for my lack of progress, other excuses abounded. In the end, I couldn't proceed until I chose to invest the required effort, and I wasn't yet ready to make that decision.

Streets provided a much more difficult challenge. I had just mastered the smooth, level tile floors at the hospital. Now I faced bumps, rough surfaces, and hills. The smallest incline often defeated me; sometimes even the crowned shape of the streets seemed too extreme to overcome.

It was all just too much. I spent weeks struggling to move ten feet, and now I faced yards, blocks, and miles. Even the "wheelchair accessible" curb seemed impossibly steep and uneven. I'd press the "WALK" button, the light would change, traffic would stop, and before I could even maneuver to the curb, the cycle was over. "DON'T WALK" warned me not to cross. How could they ever expect me to get to the other side?

In Boulder, Colorado, a news story described a wheelchair user who threatened to sue the city. His complaint: the "WALK" signal didn't invite him to cross the street since he couldn't "walk." I'll confess to staring at that discouraging, blinking "DON'T WALK" at times, reflecting on the irony of its message.

In retrospect, I am astonished that any of my therapists from that time will still speak to me. I repaid their kindness and dedication with anger and hostility. They wanted to help me return to my life, but despite my obvious need for their assistance, I simply wasn't trying.

I put all my effort into being pathetic, and hoping everyone would feel sorry for me. They needed to understand the absurdity of their vision for a meaningful life. The sooner everyone accepted that we were all wasting our time, that I was irreparably broken, the sooner we could all just quit squandering our efforts.

LEONARD

I think Leonard represented a last resort for the hospital staff. They had tried everything, and everyone else. He was an experienced physical therapist new to the hospital, and I was one of his first clients.

Like the other therapists, Leonard tried multiple approaches with me. He was friendly, and we talked about sports and movies as he worked and I didn't. He encouraged and coaxed, then pushed harder and became impatient when I failed to respond. I didn't intend to be nasty or ungrateful, but I was. Like everyone else, Leonard failed to recognize the futility that was so obvious to me.

Although I didn't openly admit it, I gave up. I went through the motions, waiting for something to end this interminable nightmare. I saw no hope. Despite the encouragement of everyone around me, I simply didn't believe I could do it. Whatever "it" was, I couldn't do it.

I couldn't get stronger, go back to work, create anything resembling a normal life. I saw no future to justify any sort of effort, and I was angry with those who were oblivious to the hopelessness. How could they keep acting as if a meaningful future beckoned?

How could they tell me happily about their weekend triathlons, new love affairs, and "problems" with the plumbing at home? Couldn't they see I no longer had a life worth living? That athletics and love were no longer real for me? That their petty inconveniences were nothing compared to *my* problems? Why did they keep behaving as though anything outside the confines of this wretched chair would ever have anything to do with me?

I've learned I can achieve amazing results, probably more than even my therapists honestly believed possible. I've crossed those streets, defying the command: "DON'T WALK." I've cranked a hand cycle three thousand miles in a year. I'm a successful junior high school teacher, a role that would terrify many able-bodied people.

But when I met Leonard, none of these possibilities had even reached the "dream" stage. I was busy proving you can't accomplish anything if you don't believe.

Leonard tried for several weeks to break through my resistance. As wasted session followed wasted session, he became increasingly frustrated. In spite of my lack of effort I achieved small incidental gains, but I basically stood (or, rather, sat) still. He knew how much I needed to accomplish, and he increasingly viewed this pretend-therapy as an unproductive waste of his time. He was right.

One morning when I arrived at the hospital, Leonard waited at the entrance. He suggested we skip our morning session (fine with me!) and just take a walk. I figured he wanted to check up on me, and he was about to discover I'd made little progress toward building endurance. Of course he already knew that, but I didn't care. He needed to see for himself how impossible this all was.

Leonard had chosen a spectacular June morning in Colorado, pristine blue sky, warm and calm, a wonderful day for a walk, or a roll, if nothing else. If you were lucky enough to have a life, this would have been a great day to be alive. After Leonard stood around while I made a great show of grunting and straining to roll a few feet at a time, he offered to push the chair. "Let's get away from this place."

At last! He finally accepted that this is too hard, that I just can't do it. He really felt sorry for me.

After we traveled about four blocks we paused at the top of a hill, a location I had carefully avoided in my limited explorations of the neighborhood. I knew if I approached the precipice of this monster mountain, I'd plummet over the edge and they'd find my body at the bottom in a mangled, smoldering pile of wheelchair parts.

I recently drove to the same street, parked my truck at the top and sat peering down at the STOP sign at the bottom. I chuckled to myself; that sign would have been a fleeting memory on that distant summer day as I careened past it, probably covering my eyes with my arms to brace for the coming crash.

On that long-ago day, with Leonard at the controls, that "hill" was a double-black-diamond ski mountain lined with suburban houses. I thought of those ten one-foot tiles, smooth and level, that defeated me for so long. How could I hope to control my chair on such a dangerous slope? The quiet residential street ended at an intersection with a busy thoroughfare. What if he slipped? I would have no chance of stopping myself on such an incline.

We reached the bottom and stopped just short of the cars whizzing past the intersection. Leonard turned the chair around and pointed it up the hill. He reached down and locked the brakes.

"See you back at the hospital."

He walked away, up the mountain, without another word! Yeah, right, I thought. He's going to stop at the top of the hill and watch while I remind him that mountain climbing isn't in my therapy plan. If this is supposed to be funny, it's not. What does he think he's going to accomplish by leaving me at the bottom of this impossible ascent?

He just kept going, up the hill, over the top, out of sight, and just left me sitting there, next to all of that traffic, right in the middle of the street.

Is he crazy? I'm going to get killed!

I waited. Surely he's bluffing, just trying to scare me or make some sort of sick point about how I need to get to work.

I waited. No way he's going to just leave me here. He'll come back. He has to.

He didn't.

So there I sat. Cars screamed past on the busy street behind me, while Mount Everest loomed in front of me. How long before he returns and admits the insanity of his little stunt?

A car turned the corner, approaching from behind. Thankfully, the driver saw me and steered around, glaring at me as he passed. He probably figured that's how I ended up in a wheelchair in the first place, too stupid to stay out of traffic.

Leonard didn't reappear. He's serious! He expects me to climb this mountain by myself. He's out of his mind!

I decided I'd better try to move before a car streaked around the corner and smashed into me. I thought at least I could get closer to the curb. I released the brakes and immediately began rolling backward toward the traffic. I tried to grab the wheels to stop, but my useless hands proved no match for the incline. I released the wheels and quickly set the brakes to halt my backward roll toward disaster.

Now what? After that failed effort, I was even closer to traffic. Another attempt like that and I'd be in the middle of the busy street.

I tried again, slower this time. I released the brakes, and grabbed the wheels before I started rolling. It worked! I could hold my position on this monster slope! Let's celebrate; someone come get me and we'll have a party.

I'd managed to successfully sit still. But move forward? No way; the slope was just too steep. I locked the brakes. Safe again—sort of. But now what? I'm going to die right here at the base of this hill, and probably starve to death if a car doesn't hit me first. They'll discover my skeleton slumped in a rusty wheelchair.

Obviously, Leonard was not coming back, so after a few minutes I decided I'd better try again. Now I had the first part mastered—release the brakes, grab the wheels. No backward roll. I knew this was impossible, but I pushed forward with all of the strength in my stick arms.

Hey! I actually moved maybe a foot forward. Progress! I moved my hands for another push.

Oops. My hands slipped on the rims and I rolled backward again. Quick. Brakes.

I was farther back now than when I started. Because I didn't set the brakes simultaneously, the chair had turned a bit. Now I wasn't even pointed in the right direction.

This was becoming really scary. I felt completely out of control. One more slip and I'd roll into that busy street. I was tired and hot.

I had to try to get going. I released one brake and pushed that wheel; now I was straight again. Lock the brake. Rest.

I unlocked both brakes. I was getting the hang of it, catching the wheels before I rolled backward. I'd push forward just a little, then slide my hands quickly back and catch the wheels. Success! Again. Again.

I locked the brakes. My shoulders ached, my arms burned, and I had only moved a couple of feet forward.

And so it went. Forward a little, two or three pushes, rest, two or three more, rest, then again. Halfway up this giant hill, I was finished. No more, I just can't do it. My arms felt dead. I locked the brakes, certain I couldn't go any farther. Isn't this enough? Look how far I got. Why doesn't someone stop and help?

I hope Leonard's proud of himself!

The cool morning faded as the hot sun climbed higher in the cloudless blue sky. I was exhausted, thirsty, and scared. More than anything, I was scared to death. I'd been saying for months that life wasn't worth living, but I didn't envision crashing into traffic or frying to death in the hot afternoon sun.

I learned the most valuable lesson of my entire rehab process sitting in the middle of that hill. I didn't realize it at the time, but I discovered I could do "it." I would encounter pain, fear, frustration, and failure, but I could do it. Whatever "it" was, I could do it.

I reached the top of that hill. One or two feet at a time, slowly creeping along, certain every moment I couldn't go another inch. Each hand movement involved the danger of slipping, sending me careening out of control into the traffic below. Exhausted, hot, thirsty, and tired, I made it to the top.

I turned and looked back down the hill in amazement. However, I couldn't be proud of my accomplishment because I was too busy being angry. How could Leonard have done that to me?

I still had to struggle the four blocks back to the hospital. I swear that ants on the pavement passed me as I crept along. Little old ladies on that sidewalk would have looked like NASCAR racers speeding past with their walkers. Finally, the hospital doors opened and I felt the cold rush of the air conditioning. I probably would have just sat there in the cool shade, but I was determined to find Leonard and let him know what I thought of his little stunt.

After a long visit to a drinking fountain, I pushed slowly through the halls, grateful for the familiar tile floors. The elevator was easy now, down a floor, and I reached the P.T. clinic. The receptionist greeted me with her ever-present smile, but I ignored her. Around the corner, and Leonard stood in front of me. He was talking to someone, making notes on a clipboard, laughing. Apparently he just forgot about me!

"Hey, Rich. It's good to see you. Welcome back. Wow, it's past noon. I'm hungry. Come on, I'll buy lunch."

He headed off down the hall toward the cafeteria.

Past noon? No kidding! I just cooked myself climbing that mountain while he stood in the nice cool air-conditioned hospital. Past noon? I'll tell you about "past noon."

I can't repeat what I said to his back as he disappeared. I questioned his heritage, ancestry, humanity, and fitness as a professional, among other things. He probably couldn't hear my croaking curses, since he didn't even turn around. Before I finished whispering my rehearsed speech, he disappeared through the door.

I had no intention of sharing lunch with him, but I couldn't just let him walk away. I struggled after him, down another long hall and a small incline. There he was, waiting patiently for me at the cafeteria entrance. I'd like to wipe that smile off his face. What's he so happy about?

"What do you want for lunch? My treat," he said in the most matter-of-fact manner possible. As I began again to yell, or what passed for "yelling" with my raspy voice, he calmly turned and gathered trays and silverware. He plopped a tray on my lap.

"I didn't check on the special for today. I'm just getting a burger. What do you want?"

Several folks were now in line behind us, so I postponed my tirade with a shrug. I wasn't about to play buddies with this jerk.

"OK. Burger and fries for two." Leonard collected the food and drinks, paid the tab, and walked to a table near a window. I followed, weaving through the maze of tables, still seething.

As I arrived at the table, he turned and said with a twinkle in his eye, "I didn't think you'd want to go outside for lunch today. Probably better inside where it's cool, huh?"

I couldn't help it. I wanted to be angry. I felt half-cooked, hot, and tired, and I was terrified as the traffic rushed past and one slip of my weakened hands could have sent me crashing down that hill. He could have gotten me killed!

But I couldn't help it. I failed to stifle the smile, and my anger faded as a giggle escaped. I shook my head and chuckled.

"Funny," I said, laughing harder than I had since my accident. "Real funny."

He unloaded the trays, helped me to organize the food and open ketchup and mustard so I wouldn't make a mess. The burger still challenged my fumbling hands, and much of it ended up in pieces on the tray. It didn't matter. We ate and talked about hospital construction, sports, politics, with an occasional pause to gawk as a lovely lady passed our table.

Nothing said about what happened. He resisted saying *I told you so*, no de-briefing to be sure I got the point. He didn't demand a resolution, *Now are you finally going to get to work?* He didn't even remind me to be proud of my accomplishment. No one overhearing our conversation would have guessed at the significance of the moment.

Leonard and I never talked of that day. I always wondered if he actually deserted me. I sometimes suspect he was sneaking around, hiding behind trees, making sure I didn't get hurt. But I don't know and I never asked. Doesn't matter. I wouldn't believe him anyway.

Leonard gave me a priceless gift that day; he set me on the road to rediscovering self-respect. I could do "it." If I could get myself up that hill, I couldn't ever again believe myself when "I can't" threatened to defeat me.

In a movie or self-help book, my therapy would have magically turned around that afternoon. The light finally appeared. I realized the need for hard work and recognized the endless possibilities that lay ahead. I stopped complaining, found ways to work past pain. I believed I could accomplish whatever I wanted. I never again said, "I can't."

But this wasn't Hollywood and I wasn't an inspirational character in a fictional story. I struggled home that day, complaining of how hot and tired I felt, and I don't imagine there was much visible alteration in my work ethic in the days that followed.

But there was a real internal difference that changed everything. I had conquered a mountain. Not a figurative, imaginary, metaphorical mountain, but a real, live mountain! Not a contrived, antiseptic mountain in the hospital, but an impossible, overwhelming, there's-no-way-I-can-do-this mountain.

I sat at the bottom with no possibility of reaching the top. No experience, no help with technique, no safety net. No companion to step in if I started and couldn't finish. No data that said I was physically capable. No assistant to rescue me if I fell.

For the first time in more than six months, I was on my own in the world. No nurses or therapists. No guarantees I would be OK. I was a real, live, thirty-seven-year-old man—moving forward, solving problems, doing life.

Just like everybody else!

I encountered a seemingly endless series of overwhelming physical challenges in the months and years that followed. I learned to transfer to and from a car, and eventually began to drive with hand controls. I improvised routines for dressing myself, which an occupational therapist at a world-famous rehab center told me I'd never be able to accomplish independently. I relearned how to manage every detail of my life, big and small, always wanting to say, *I just can't do this one. I know I've done a lot, but this is just too much.*

I've learned to use tools and technology to make tasks easier, safer, and more efficient. I've learned to ask for and accept help—most of the time, anyway. I still have some work to do with that.

But mostly I've learned there aren't many important mountains I can't climb. I've understood the reality that fear, uncertainty, frustration, and occasionally even failure are all part of the package. I've learned that every time I say, "I can't," I'm absolutely right. But I've also learned that when I try, when I get past frustration and embarrassment, I can find ways to accomplish most tasks.

Imagine that before my injury, I could do ten thousand things. Now I can do only eight thousand. I can choose to focus on the two thousand I lost, or on the eight thousand that remain.

Leonard started me on the path toward discovering, appreciating and celebrating those eight thousand things.

Two summers after that day, I traveled to Miami for treatment at the Miami Project to Cure Paralysis, and I returned there each summer for five years. Those trips were difficult. I dealt with airports, taxis, hotels, and public transportation.

The last time I went to Miami, I registered at a hotel several miles from the clinic and stayed by myself for two weeks. I took the train each day to the hospital, and went out for dinner at night. In a quiet park near my hotel some young guys played basketball, and I watched their game and visited with them. I explored a bit of downtown and went to a beautiful outdoor mall called Bayside.

I enjoyed that trip.

Those were all things I thought impossible, as impossible as climbing that suburban mountain on a warm summer day. None of it was easy. I've had to learn a bit of patience, to accept that many routine tasks take longer. But my final trip to Miami represented a big step in the journey that began at the bottom of that hill.

Many people had *taken* care of me; Leonard cared for me. He didn't take responsibility for me. He didn't protect me. He didn't make sure it would turn out right. I *was* in real danger on that hill. I could have fallen or been hit by a car. He took a tremendous risk; if I'd been injured, he probably would have gotten in trouble. Even if he was hiding behind fences, he couldn't have stopped me from tumbling from my chair or crashing backward down the hill.

He cared for me.

I believe Leonard's incredibly wise choice that day, to risk leaving me to make it or not make it by myself, was a decision guided by the hand of God. My prayer had been to be left alone, to just die and put an end to the misery. But God knew better. He knew what I really needed, and as always, He provided.

I needed to know about possibilities I couldn't even imagine, that I could accomplish goals that weren't even thinkable, that the limitations that confronted me at every turn could be overcome. I needed to know I could climb a mountain.

God didn't answer my prayers by giving me what I asked for. He knew better, and He answered as He always does by meeting my needs rather than satisfying my desires. He sent Leonard to provide one more piece of the hope I needed to move forward.

IS THIS WHO I THINK IT IS?

Somehow I did move forward.

Slowly, in small, agonizing stages, I re-entered the world. How did I ever get back to "real life"? A good deal of difference separated "real" and what I once thought was "normal."

How in the world could I ever explain to her that "normal" now means a wheelchair, a cycle I pedal with my arms, and hand controls for driving? That "real life" includes ramps, asking for help with some of the simplest tasks, and figuring out new ways to be a teacher?

Only a junior high teacher could think of working with adolescents as "real life."

CHAPTER 11

BACK TO SCHOOL

Prior to my accident, I taught mathematics in a junior high school. Now, more than eighteen months after falling on my head and losing the use of most of my body, I once again encountered a new group of young teenagers. I had anticipated the first day of school more than fifteen times before, but the beginning of this school year was different.

Miraculously, I had regained most of the use of my arms. My hands worked a little, the right a bit better than the left. I could move the toes slightly on both feet, but essentially I was still paralyzed below my chest. I recovered feeling and sensation everywhere, though it wasn't entirely normal. I could feel touch and pressure, but hot/cold and sharp/dull didn't register below my chest and on portions of my arms and hands.

My accident caused what's known as an "incomplete" spinal cord injury, meaning my spinal cord wasn't severed. Instead, bruising damaged the spinal nerves, probably caused by swelling in the minutes and hours after the injury.

I greeted this new group of youngsters with a voice that was much stronger than the hoarse whisper created during the spinal fusion. Two amazing surgical procedures helped my vocal cords function, but my voice still wasn't normal. Would I be able to communicate with a room full of energetic adolescents?

I sat in my wheelchair. How would kids react to a teacher who couldn't stand? I'd learned the basics of life with paralysis, and now came the next test in reconstructing my life: Could I return to work?

Could I still manage a classroom? Since the injury I had been almost completely isolated in controlled environments at home, in the hospital, and in therapy clinics. Could I adapt successfully in this area of "the real world"?

I was terrified. Could I possibly summon the energy required to do all of this? Lesson planning, conducting classes, grading, and the myriad of small tasks that comprise my profession—just a few short months ago I couldn't turn over in bed by myself. Now this group of fresh young faces looked to me for direction, as though I had any clue how to be their teacher. I wondered if they could see the fear as I struggled to keep my emotions under control and pretended I knew what to do.

I felt their uneasiness. They got much quieter than normal as they entered the room, sharing my uncertainty about what to expect. Who is this guy? What's with the wheelchair? Does he know what he's doing? What will this class be like?

Some of the kids knew the story, but for most of them this was just the first day of school and I was another teacher to figure out. They were more concerned with who sat next to them and how much homework their new math class would require than with how I ended up in this wheelchair.

The bell signaled the start of the first class, and I was supposed to do something. I had rehearsed this moment over and over, sitting alone in this familiar classroom, but now I was totally unsure. The whole idea was crazy; I was not nearly ready. How did I let my principal talk me into thinking I could pull off this act? Yeah, I climbed a hill more than a year ago, but this was different. They all waited, staring at me. I had to get class started, but suddenly my plans deserted me. What should I do first?

Call role, that's a safe way to start. Thirty pairs of eyes stared as I struggled self-consciously to pick up a pen and fumbled to mark the attendance sheet. Now we knew who was here, and I gave the kids an activity to complete. They welcomed the assignment, grateful for a diversion from the unspoken questions circling the room. Students worked together and I began moving among them, rolling uncertainly between desks, acting like it was just another first day while the fear knotted my stomach. Should I say something about the chair and about my injury? How long could we pretend there's really nothing different about this initial class?

One boy looked up as I passed his desk. In the honest, unassuming manner only a thirteen-year-old could manage, he announced, "I think I'm going to like being in your class."

"Oh yeah? Why is that?"

"Because," he said with a grin, "I hate it when teachers stand and look over my shoulder."

Right then, I knew. As I chuckled and shook my head at his little joke, I knew it was going to be all right. I moved on, commenting a little now on student work, making small talk. The atmosphere in the room lightened a bit, students talking to each other and to me, the first day of the new school year underway. Somehow, everything was going to be OK.

I should remember that young man's name. I don't, but I think about him every year as I greet another new group of students. Each year, for nineteen years now, I've wondered a bit about the reaction of each new group to a wheelchair and a teacher who writes in what we affectionately refer to as "Chinese Hieroglyphics." Every year I remember that first day, the uncertainty, the uneasy quiet, and the silly one-liner that dissolved my fear and eased the tension. Each year, as I prepare for a fresh collection of new faces, I chuckle to myself, knowing it'll all be OK somehow.

I've learned to adapt. Technology helped, along with a bit of specially designed furniture and some experience with what's effective. I've learned that, just like everyone else, I can take advantage of the many things I do well and that I have to find ways to overcome weaknesses. I've learned after a lot of pain and struggle to enjoy my own corny sense of humor, to laugh at myself, and to take it all a little less seriously.

That young man's joke helped me realize it's better to chuckle than to complain. I've learned that my students, like most other folks, see a person more than they see a person in a wheelchair. I've learned that my kids, like most people, care a lot more about how they're treated than whether I stand or sit.

I smiled as I recalled an event from earlier that morning, one of many seemingly small memories that form the foundation of this life I've managed to reconstruct. I sat in my empty classroom, overwhelmed by uncertainty, wishing I could run away, certain that this was too much to expect. As I sought an escape from the insanity, a young lady appeared in the doorway.

"Hi, I'm Megan," she announced as she strode boldly into the room. I knew this girl. She was my friend Liz's daughter, a new seventh grader at our school.

"Hi, Megan. What can I do for you?"

"I want to know if I can get you a cup of coffee." Liz knew I liked coffee in the morning, but the staff lounge was quite a distance from my room and up a ramp that was still too steep for my stick-arms. Coffee had been the farthest thing from my mind as I tried to calm my fear that morning.

"Yeah, that would be really nice."

"OK." She opened the cabinet where my cups had been stored since the accident, grabbed one, and headed out the door. In a few minutes she was back and I had my customary morning coffee. One small piece of "normal" had materialized in the midst of the chaos, something familiar in this strange new world.

"Thanks, Megan. This was really nice of you."

"You're welcome," she smiled. "See you tomorrow morning."

I saw her the next morning, and every morning for the next three years. Megan took her self-appointed job seriously. For three years she spilled coffee on her shoes while descending a short flight of stairs.

Whenever she was absent, she made sure her mom remembered to get my coffee. And when she finally left for high school, she trained her little brother Aaron to take over for the next three years.

How remarkable that such a small act of kindness meant so much as I tried to find my bearings and adapt to all that was so new and different. And even more amazing that now, nineteen years later, I again greet Megan each morning as she unlocks the door that joins my classroom to the one in which she teaches. Who could have guessed that the little girl who eased my fear all those years ago by greeting me each morning with a smile and a cup of coffee would become a colleague and fellow math teacher? I don't even make her fetch coffee anymore. She'd probably still spill it on her shoes.

Each year, a new young person volunteers for the honored position of "Mr. D's coffee kid." Nineteen new groups of students—I've helped them learn a bit of math, and they've helped me to get my life back.

I am quite sure that I got the better end of the deal.

IS THIS WHO I THINK IT IS?

I didn't even drink coffee twenty years ago. Church classes and morning meetings did that to me.

How would the answer to this question appear if I had tried to get through all of this without help? I recalled with gratitude the incredible people who appeared on the path when I was most in need.

CHAPTER 12

THREE WISE GUYS

Being back at school changed my physical activity, but my defeatist attitude persisted. A dreary routine of work and therapy evolved, driven more by survival than hope. I hate to imagine how much money my insurance company paid for marginally beneficial physical therapy. The therapists worked hard, but mostly I still just went through the motions. I became an accomplished complainer and excuse-maker.

So many names come to mind during my five months in the hospital: Julie, Lilly, Greg, Joyce, Kathleen. Leonard and Ruth during the years of outpatient rehab, and many others whose names my aging brain has long forgotten. They knew what I needed, but they couldn't make me believe. As long as I remained convinced that this part-of-a-life was hopeless, I couldn't take advantage of the essential help these dedicated people wanted so badly to provide.

My intensely stubborn resistance defies explanation. After heaven, the monster, and the mountain, I still turned away from the support God so faithfully placed along my path. People and experiences continually appeared in my life as God waited for me to surrender. God patiently offered hope, but I refused to accept it.

That's the story of *Relentless Grace*. God never quit on me. Even as I actively sabotaged my recovery, God built a foundation of hope on which I could depend. He knew my needs and, as He always does, He fulfilled them and waited for me to claim the second chance He offers to each of us.

So I still went to the hospital for pretend-therapy and undermined the incredibly positive approach and expertise offered by Ruth, my last therapist. We seemed to have a sort of unspoken agreement: she did all she could to help me get better while I complained and put forth as little effort as possible. She pushed, I resisted. She believed in possibilities, I believed that nothing worthwhile could emerge from a shattered body trapped in a wheelchair.

A year or so after I went back to work, Ruth announced that I should learn to walk. I'd done some standing exercises in what's called a "standing frame," a mechanical device that lifted and supported me in a standing position. This weight-bearing activity strengthened my bones, and the upright posture forced improved circulation and encouraged muscle development in my abdomen and back. Standing also allowed me to view the world from a different perspective.

Like everything else, I did this work half-heartedly. I'd stand for a few brief moments and quickly sit down, complaining about being light-headed or nauseous or whatever other excuse I could imagine. Another potentially healthy activity yielded minimal benefits because I just didn't try.

I thought Ruth had lost her mind when she said I was ready to walk. I usually figured she knew what she was talking about since she had prior experience working with spinal cord injuries. But the whole point of paralysis was that walking wasn't going to happen. It didn't seem like you'd need a degree in physical therapy to understand what was painfully clear to me: "legs don't move" equals "no walking."

This new craziness, however, seemed to make perfect sense to everyone else, so I resigned myself to not-trying walking as I had not-tried everything else. A prosthetics specialist appeared at my next session to measure me for a set of leg braces.

Space-age technology merged with Dark-age restraint to fashion these newest instruments of torture. Each brace consisted of two steel rods connected somehow to a pair of heavy shoes. Special hinges locked my knees in place to mimic a standing position. A complex series of padded cuffs and straps with Velcro fastenings secured the braces at my knee and upper thigh.

I couldn't attach these contraptions by myself, so Ruth and an aide strapped them to my lifeless legs. It took both of them to hoist me into a standing posture and lock the hinges. They placed a four-legged walker in front of me so I could lean on my arms, and I stood independently for the first time in more than two years. It should have been an exciting moment of liberation.

My weak arms tired quickly as I leaned heavily on the walker. Useless abdominal and back muscles couldn't stabilize my hips, and only my helpers' grip on a belt secured around my waist, kept me upright. My sway-backed posture placed painful stress on my lower back.

I could "stand" for only a few minutes. Leaning forward on my arms compressed my chest and restricted breathing. Ruth and her assistant lowered me into my wheelchair, and I struggled to breathe and clear my head. Then we repeated the process, again and again, moments of standing and dizziness, then sitting, then upright once more.

After several repetitions of this process, Ruth decided I was ready to try a "step." I searched for a balance point and scooted the walker ahead a few inches. Then I leaned forward, pushed up with my arms, and tried to lift myself and swing my feet forward.

I may have moved an inch, a disappointing baby step that didn't get much better with non-practice. Complaining constantly, I dragged myself around the gym inches at a time, stopping every few steps to sit and recover.

After a few weeks of non-improvement, Ruth announced a plan to increase the frequency and intensity of my non-walking. The pre-physical therapy curriculum at Colorado State University required several hours of volunteer work, so she arranged for a student to assist with my "walking." We agreed to meet at my home for a training session.

Shane appeared on the porch a few minutes before Ruth arrived. He was a big guy and seemed genuinely interested in helping. He asked insightful questions, obviously an intelligent young man with a passion for his future profession. He already knew a lot about my injury, and he was anxious to apply classroom principles. Shane seemed like a nice enough person, but his eager anticipation was one-sided.

Ruth arrived. She showed Shane how to attach the braces, safely lift me, and hold me steady as I dragged myself along. He was a natural for this work, combining physical strength with a kind, gentle manner.

Shane came to my house a few times each week for more than a year before he graduated, and we became good friends. He was a weight-lifter, and because he worked out so much, it was a bit embarrassing to complain and make excuses when he was helping me. I wish I could claim amazing gains, but at best I worked just a little harder than before. When I wanted to skip my exercise with claims of pain, exhaustion or a simple lack of motivation, he found ways to keep me going.

After he graduated from college, Shane tried for several years to get into physical therapy school. He almost gave up a couple of times, but his persistence was rewarded when he entered the highly selective P.T. program at the University of Colorado School of Medicine. I suspect many people have benefited from his skills, patience, and gentle spirit.

I really missed him when he moved away. I didn't realize how much his quiet confidence impacted me. My physical progress may have been minimal, but his friendship meant more than I imagined. He was one of the few people from whom I didn't isolate myself, and he provided an empathetic ear at a time when I refused to talk to anyone else.

A few weeks later, another student offered to take over as my walking partner. I was reluctant to allow a new assistant into my life, but I wasn't able to concoct a good excuse to decline.

Bruce provided quite a change of pace. Shane was a former football player. Bruce played soccer and was significantly smaller than his predecessor. Shane was something of a free spirit; Bruce was quieter and more serious, however, they also had a lot in common. Bruce had the same intelligence, gentle manner, and desire to help. Despite his smaller stature, he could easily lift me and help with my "walking."

I doubted whether Bruce could possibly replace Shane, and I was right. You don't "replace" friends, but new people bring different qualities and dimensions that fill out and enrich your life. At first I missed the friendly banter that had become part of the walking sessions with Shane, but Bruce and I eventually developed a great friendship.

Bruce helped me with my walking for two years, and at times I made quite a bit of progress. His serious nature translated into our work together, and he was impatient with my lack of effort. He pushed more than Shane did, and for some reason I didn't reject his coaching.

I suspect that I mostly responded to his commitment, his willingness to show up several times per week long after he had fulfilled his volunteer requirement. Bruce continued to help for one reason—he cared. That commitment changed my life.

When Bruce graduated, he needed a break from school. He moved to California and gained a valuable year of experience as an aide in a physical therapy clinic. He returned to his studies in an elite program at St. Louis University.

Both of these young men gave so much and asked nothing in return. They freely and cheerfully volunteered countless hours of their time along with valuable support, assistance, and knowledge. Most importantly, they offered friendship at a time when I wasn't particularly easy to befriend. They got credit for the volunteer time, and I suppose they learned a bit from the experience. If nothing else, they learned a good deal about the frustration of trying to help someone who really didn't want to be helped.

But I'm quite sure I got the better end of the bargain. As with so many of the people who tried to help, I didn't fully appreciate what they did for me. It's difficult to imagine how the process might have turned out if they hadn't been so committed to my recovery. I miss both of them.

Both Shane and Bruce made considerable efforts to maintain contact, but I was too busy being depressed and pitiful to reciprocate. I did attend Shane's wedding, and I received an invitation to Bruce's wedding but didn't reply. Eventually, after I didn't respond to their letters and cards, they stopped writing. My loss. I deeply regret my unwillingness to maintain contact with those two wonderful young men.

After Bruce left, I was certain I wouldn't find another acceptable assistant. I had been extremely fortunate to encounter two amazing volunteers, and I couldn't believe I'd find another student with the ability to help me and tolerate my nasty attitude.

I was wrong.

Bruce's departure provided a good excuse to avoid the work for a few months. Standing in the braces was really uncomfortable because of the stress on my lower back, and my version of walking wouldn't ever provide a useful way to get around. Getting the braces on and off, struggling into position, and locking the knee joints was impossible for me to accomplish independently. Besides, without assistance I would quickly lose my balance and fall.

So "walking" was really just a form of healthy, beneficial exercise. I wasn't about to get excited about an activity simply because it might actually help me get better. So I wasn't thrilled when I discovered that a third student had volunteered for the thankless position as my assistant.

Tom was not quite what I expected when I opened my front door. Shane was a big, burly, outgoing teddy bear of a guy. Bruce was compact, tough, and quietly intense. Tom was—different.

Tall and skinny, with an unruly mop of curly hair, he greeted me with the goofy grin of a kid meeting his girlfriend's dad for the first time. Behind him, parked on the street, I could see an old blue and white VW microbus that had seen better days. *Great,* I thought, *just what I need, a latter-day hippie.*

First impressions faded quickly. Tom easily learned the mechanics of attaching the braces, hoisting me into position, and keeping me steady as I dragged lifeless feet around my house. He quickly developed a good sense of what I was supposed to accomplish and offered helpful ideas that would have made a difference if I had actually been trying to improve. He knew a lot about my injury. I realized there was a good deal more to this silly college kid than I had first suspected.

Tom demonstrated a real aptitude for analyzing my odd walking motion. I'd slide the walker forward, then lean, press up with my arms, and swing my legs forward. On the rare occasions when I did a few steps at a time, I'd sometimes establish a rhythm and move a few feet before stopping. Within a couple of sessions he determined an adjustment for the braces that relieved some of the stress on my lower back and made standing a little less uncomfortable. He was an experienced bicycle mechanic, and soon he began to maintain and adjust my wheelchair.

I also discovered that Tom shared my affinity for bad humor and practical jokes. As I dragged myself along, he distracted me with corny one-liners and tales of pranks perpetrated by his housemates. Bruce and Shane had become good friends; Tom and I formed a bond that bridged the twenty-year gap in our ages. I began to look forward to Tom's visits in spite of the work they involved. For the first time since my accident, I was having fun, laughing, and I was actually working at my therapy. The goofy kid with that ridiculous crop of hair accomplished what had been impossible for nurses, therapists, and friends. He penetrated the barrier of self-pity and hopelessness.

Like Shane and Bruce before him, Tom graduated and moved away after a couple of years, however, he traveled a less conventional path. Unlike my first two volunteer assistants, Tom decided not to apply to a physical therapy school. He would have been a tremendous therapist. His intelligence, strength, and caring spirit would surely have made him a success in that challenging profession.

Jimmy Buffet wrote a song about a friend who ". . . just couldn't find his occupation in the twentieth century." That's kind of how things have gone for Tom since he graduated. He worked in a bicycle shop in Denver for a while, then returned to Fort Collins. He's worked at a couple of different jobs while searching for his vocation.

In more than a decade since he first appeared at my door with that silly grin, Tom has been one of my best and most valued friends. He has been my wheelchair mechanic, landscaper, furniture mover, painter, baseball game companion, chess opponent, and Christmas tree decorator. He helped me get started riding my first hand cycle and has been my faithful cycle mechanic for seven years.

While Tom continues to seek his profession, now in the twenty-first century, I benefit from his friendship, support, and constant positive approach to life. In our ten years relationship the practical jokes have diminished but not disappeared, and we both have a lot less hair. But Tom's goofy smile and the loving spirit remain.

I cannot possibly summarize the impact of these three young men. Shane, Bruce, and Tom exemplified compassion, caring, and a passion for enriching the lives of others. They volunteered to help because of a course requirement. They changed my life through their commitment and love.

Three more times, God provided. In spite of my inability to believe anything of worth could be found within this broken life, God was working within the painful circumstances of my injury to create something greater than I could imagine.

Even in the face of my resistance and failure to accept His promises, He continued to provide. As always, it wasn't about my lack of faith, but about His perfect faithfulness.

It took me a long time to realize all of this. But Shane, Bruce, and Tom, the three wise guys, surely helped me to move in the right direction. I'm deeply thankful to all three of them.

IS THIS WHO I THINK IT IS?

Even after so much time and apparent progress, I wasn't even close to being prepared to move forward. I still didn't have any idea how to approach this damaged new life I'd been handed. I was surviving, but I certainly had no answer to "who this is."

There was much yet to discover. Once again, God sent just the right person, a most unlikely guide for an essential and difficult part of the journey.

It was time to dig up the artifacts of a life that was broken long before an unfortunate accident highlighted the damage. I didn't know it at the time, but that excavation would take me back twenty years.

How would I ever explain to her how I reached the moment when I pressed *send* and launched the message that prompted her inscrutable question?

CHAPTER 13

PETE

"Tell me again—why can't you contact her?"

Pete had that therapist's ability to ask a dumb question and make it sound perfectly reasonable. The notion of contacting Becky after nearly twenty years was completely crazy. Anyone with an ounce of common sense could create a long list of reasons why intruding into her life after so much time, after everything that had happened, was a really bad idea. Why was it so difficult to understand why I couldn't open all of those old wounds for her? Why did he keep asking the same ridiculous question?

I explained once again what should have been apparent to a guy who was supposed to be an expert in human relationships. Time and again our conversations cycled back to the topic of "Becky," and each time he'd ask the same stupid question. Then he'd listen as I repeated my explanation of what should have been obvious. He'd smile and nod, and we'd move on.

Over and over, month after month, as we sifted through the chaos of my life, we'd return to the same dialogue like actors rehearsing an important scene they couldn't get quite right. He'd ask, I'd explain, and he'd smile. "Oh, yeah," he'd say. "That's why," as though he finally got it. Except that he never did.

I wondered what motivated this absurd, ever-present question. What was he really asking? He couldn't possibly believe that contacting her made any sense, so what was the point of returning again and again to such a pointless inquiry? What was really bouncing around in his psychologist brain?

I didn't want to talk to a counselor anyway. Immediately after the injury, people began to suggest I talk to someone about what had happened and get some help dealing with all the issues I faced. I stubbornly refused. I had a degree in counseling; I didn't need anyone else to help me pretend to make sense of a situation that made no sense at all. I was miserable, and there was nothing a counselor or anyone else was going to do to alter the situation.

I wallowed in intense depression. As I continued to deny my obvious need, I was in an emotional free fall. I was mean and nasty to everyone around me, angrily rejecting all efforts by others to help me adjust to the difficult life that confronted me. In spite of my lack of commitment, I made minimal physical progress. But mentally I spiraled deeper into a seemingly bottomless well of anger, depression, and isolation that grew exponentially as I made life miserable for family and friends who were trying so hard to help.

My anger destroyed nearly every close relationship in my life, including my second marriage. We'd been married for a bit more than two years when I fell. Despite consistent efforts to offer support, I refused to display anything beyond anger, resentment, and pessimism. I couldn't acknowledge that the accident impacted the lives of everyone who cared about me and that those closest were affected the most. My refusal to deal with the depression created an impossible situation. I was determined to prove there was no hope. The more she tried to assist, the more I claimed I wanted to be left alone. Eventually I got my wish.

I continued to hear the same suggestion: Why don't you talk to someone? I dismissed the notion while I scrambled to maintain some sort of emotional equilibrium. I was in survival mode at work, barely able to summon the energy and focus required to deal with 150 teenagers each day. I was supposed to exercise after work, but the determination required just to get through the day was overwhelming. I was drowning in despair, physical pain, and loneliness as I endured a wretched present and a future devoid of hope.

Still, I persisted—I didn't need to talk to any counselor.

As I reflect on those horrible years, an obvious question arises: Where was God during all of this? What about all of that grace and forgiveness stuff? Why wasn't I praying, reading the Bible, and clinging tightly to the promises of this personal God in whom I claimed to believe? What happened to Jesus as I suffered in fear and depression? What good was this faith of mine if it failed to show up when I needed it most?

Where was *hope*?

Good questions, and I don't have good answers. My church family reached out again and again, but I rejected their overtures with increasing bitterness. My friend Al transferred to another state, and my disappointment over the circumstances of his departure became my pretense for not attending church any longer. I continued to withdraw and isolate myself from every source of support.

I still believed in God, and I prayed, and I had faith in Jesus as my Savior. But I had no idea how faith and prayer might mitigate the never-ending crisis in which impossible issues bombarded me from all directions. I never blamed God for my accident, because thankfully I knew better, but I had no clue how to lean on Him and allow His love and His people to carry me through this ordeal.

I seemed to think God was over there, while my pain and misery were over here, and one somehow had little to do with the other. I continued to talk to God, but I had no idea I could let go of all of this striving and failing, give the whole awful mess to Him, and trust that He would make something good from what I could only perceive as a lost cause.

I was in fact a "baby Christian." In the six years between that night on the church steps and my accident, I thought I'd grown a lot in my faith. I suppose I progressed significantly from the point at which I began, but my Christianity was still pretty close to the surface. I'd been active in church and learned a lot about the basics of the Bible story. I'd become quite accomplished at appearing to know what all this stuff was about.

But what I understood was mostly just Bible knowledge. I hadn't applied any of it in any significant way to my life. I was a student who listened to the lectures, read the text superficially, and learned what was required to pass the exam. I never really made any sense of the material. I hadn't internalized it, challenged it, or analyzed it in any depth. I knew the words, but they were mostly the words of others.

Now, at the most difficult moment of my life, I tried desperately to synthesize a complex mass of subtle concepts—pain, love, loss, redemption, guilt, forgiveness, good, evil, hope, faith—into some sort of coherent structure that could help me create anything positive from the ruins of my life. My Christianity consisted entirely of "head knowledge" and I needed to convert it to "heart knowledge."

Of course, that's precisely why I needed guidance. As I continued to deny what was so clear to everyone else, insisting I could contend with a devastating situation by myself, my sense of futility produced a self-ordained cycle of disappointment. The more lost I became, the harder I tried to discover logic in circumstances where none existed. Failure deepened my depression, and I became even more desperate for some kind of resolution I was supposed to know how to construct. So I spun around and around, deeper and deeper, more and more hopeless.

My unrealistic strategy was destined to implode. I attempted to si-multaneously complete a graduate course in theology, with insufficient background and no instruction, while I adapted to a radically altered reality without any assistance. At the same time, I expected to self-diag-nose and treat significant psychological maladies, all the while seeking to integrate the entire mess into coherent internal significance.

I was correct about one aspect of my insane approach. I insisted that this part-of-a-life I'd been handed was hopeless, and indeed it was.

The downward spiral I created was a collision course with disaster. The crash was inevitable.

I'm not certain about the source of my conviction that I was expected to create sense from nonsense. I may as well have attempted to spin gold from straw. What psychological or emotional deficiency fashioned the notion that I should not feel powerless, angry, or resentful in the face of a devastating injury, and that I was supposed to know how to banish such crippling emotions? Why did I conclude I ought to know how to manufacture good from circumstances clearly rooted in evil?

I suppose I could analyze and speculate about the basis for such impossible standards, but I'm not sure any of that matters. What does matter is that I eventually understood the futility of my attempt to discover virtue where it didn't exist.

The Bible says it clearly: God works for good in all things. It's not my job! God will work for good, even when evil twists and perverts the good He intends. I didn't have to know how to make senseless events make sense. That's God's job, and He's never going to give up. Even in the broken body and shattered dreams of a life devoid of hope, God can and will work for good. He creates hope where none exists. Even when I cannot find the faith to trust, when I refuse to try, God is always with me and He will always work for good. He will not quit. That's what *Relentless Grace* is all about.

In retrospect, it's clear to me that God was right there all along. I'm certain Jesus wept with me, felt every bit of the pain and fear, and stood beside me when all I could see was loss and grief. God was at work from those first terrible moments, ready to bring good from the terrible tangle my life had become.

When I saw bleakness, God envisioned a life of hope and fulfillment. At the lowest times, when I rejected everyone He sent to help, God provided. And when I finally reached the end of my ability to resist, God sent Pete to guide me from the darkness.

On a night when I could go no further and struggle no more, when the only thing I could imagine to end the madness was dying, and I knew I could not accomplish that either, God provided. Years after my injury, years of anger and fear and bitterness, I finally let go. As I sat alone, weary, lost, at the end of my proverbial rope and without the will to tie a knot, God provided yet again.

Pete entered my life in a rather mundane manner. No angel or streams of light proclaimed his ordination as my guide through the grim circumstances that now comprised my life. His name was unremarkable among many in the yellow pages; nothing spectacular recommended it over the others, not the first or the largest, no color or bold print distinguished it, no heavenly starlight directed my search. But as I scanned the listings in quiet desperation that late night, Pete's ad caught my eye.

I started to dial a few others but lost my nerve. What do I say? How do I ask a stranger for this kind of support? I'd press a few numbers uncertainly with my right thumb, hesitate, and hang up. I can't do this, but I *have* to, so I'd try another, hesitate again and give up.

I punched the first digits in Pete's ad, paused—and completed the number. I didn't think of it at the time, but later I wondered why I overcame the indecision. How did I know he was the right guy? Why didn't I hang up when the machine answered?

God works in the ordinary events of our lives. When I was finally ready to listen, to surrender, to reach out, He provided an answer. Accident or fate did not direct my reply to Pete's recorded greeting.

The machine asked me to leave a message and promised a return call as soon as possible. Great. I finally wanted more than anything to talk to somebody, and now I'd have to wait until tomorrow, because it was obviously too late to return messages tonight. So I left my name and number and mumbled something about why I wanted to see him.

A few minutes later, the phone startled me. I fumbled to pick up the receiver. "Hello?"

"Hi, is this Rich?"

"Yeah." Who in the world would be calling this late?

PETE

"Hi, Rich. My name is Pete. You left a message a few minutes ago. What's up?"

Where do I begin? How do I convey the disarray and hopelessness to a stranger on the other end of the phone line? What do I say? He listened for a few moments as I outlined the story for him, recounting the facts dispassionately in contrast to the desperation and turmoil swirling inside.

As I finished my tale, the phone was quiet. Then Pete spoke softly. "Wow. You've had a rough time. Sounds like we need to get together."

We talked briefly about schedules, and he promised to call tomorrow after trying to rearrange a couple of appointments. I had resisted for so long, and now I wanted desperately just to keep talking, to dump the whole sordid mess on someone else and gain some relief and peace. I didn't want to wait for an appointment. I couldn't face another night of turmoil. I tried almost desperately to keep him on the phone. I had finally reached out, and now I wanted to cling to this initial glimmer of hope.

The call ended much too quickly.

I met Pete a couple of days later. I had enough time since that late-night phone call to have a lot of second thoughts, wonder why I was here, and dredge up all the reasons why this wouldn't accomplish anything. What could this guy do to make the nightmare end? But I was also certain I could not keep going any longer without something changing. Somehow, some way, I needed help.

I don't recall the details of my first conversation with Pete, and I don't remember much about our weekly meetings over the next months. While the particulars of those encounters are lost, I retain a sense that I began to emerge from the darkness. In steps so small they can only be perceived while retracing the path, I examined a life seemingly devoid of meaning and joy. As Pete listened and guided, I exposed and confronted struggles old and new. He encouraged me to write, and the words poured onto my keyboard as years of pain and loss flooded my heart.

I can't mentally retrace the path Pete and I traveled through the darkness. I'm not certain of the precise route we followed, how we proceeded from that night when I reached out from the edge of despair. No logical progression marks the trail to here from there. But gradually, as weeks passed into months, the darkness began to fade.

No moment of epiphany signified the magic day when everything was all right; no linear progression marked a trail from broken to whole. I gaze backward on a meandering track outlined only by slow, uncertain, but unmistakable growth and a developing belief that this jumble of a life could be sorted out. Desperation diminished and something new slowly appeared in its place, a fresh awareness so unfamiliar that I nearly failed to recognize it.

For the first time since my injury, I gave hope a chance to shine its light into the shadows and dispel the gloom that shrouded me in despair.

I didn't achieve the quick, mystical resolution essential to the uplifting ending of the inspirational TV miniseries. Old habits persisted and darkness still loomed, prepared to surround me whenever I encountered frustration or disappointment. A couple of times I pronounced myself "cured" and wandered off into the night again, including another desperate, ill-advised attempt at marriage for which I was hopelessly unprepared.

I returned when I realized I had progressed only enough to know I didn't yet know enough. No longer content to wander aimlessly, I entered a different sort of self-fulfilling spiral. Each faint flicker of hope fostered more courage to examine the issues that defined the edges of the darkness. Examination produced additional illumination, and in the new light, the darkness receded and optimism shined a bit brighter.

There's no such thing as too much darkness. When light and dark collide, light always wins. Even the smallest glimmer of hope penetrates total blackness and encourages exploration. Each small forward step forces darkness to recede and casts light into formerly fearsome recesses. Darkness only prevails where light is ignored.

I finally stopped running from the light of hope. Turning away from the shadow of depression denied its power. Each ray of hope defeated another small corner previously ruled by fear.

This new cycle pointed toward life and growth, the opposite of the death spiral in which I had been trapped for so long. I had been on a collision course with disaster; now my course indicated a more positive destiny.

This growth spiral altered the character of my writing. A rambling, confused tangle of pain, frustration, and hopelessness slowly developed into a search founded upon a sense that structure might be discovered within apparent chaos.

When I began writing in response to the counseling process, I'd arrive at each session with page after page of rambling, circular, barely coherent thoughts and feelings, artifacts of an existence in obvious turmoil even before the injury plunged me into crisis. Each week Pete patiently waded through this muddled attempt to explain the confusion. Then he smiled that ambiguous smile and encouraged me to continue writing.

I originally immersed myself in writing because of its cathartic nature. I poured pain and fear onto the pages until it seemed I had dumped the trash of my soul. Then I'd begin again, pursuing the grief like a dog chasing his tail. As I was going nowhere, pointless and apparently accomplishing nothing, until there was just no more to dump, for a short time the clanging in my head was silenced. Then the tail chasing began again, around and around and around.

As darkness receded, the writing became more lucid. I didn't write only in circles. Instead I explored, probed, searched for sense in the flood of emotions and thoughts that poured out over the weeks and months. Life gradually calmed a bit. The clamoring jumble of nonsense I had pursued in that never-ending circle seemed a little less noisy and the pursuit became a little less desperate. No longer futilely chasing my tail, I followed a faint but clear trail that began to materialize in the midst of the apparently meaningless clutter.

As with every bit of progress large or small during this journey, no miraculous leap bridged confusion to clarity, weakness to strength, tail-chasing to trail-following. I demonstrated at every stage that I'm definitely a slow learner. The track wasn't clear or easy to follow at first, but its unmistakable direction slowly became apparent.

I was traveling once again to the church steps on that quiet summer evening more than a decade ago. The sound urging me forward was the same patient voice I first heard in the whisper of the breeze in those summer trees.

"Rich, where are you?"

Now, I had a clue about what I heard and how I wished to respond.

"Here I am, Lord."

I started to read a couple of books suggested by Pete and some others that were meaningful to friends. I began to study the Bible in a manner that was new to me. Rather than reading a story, I digested small portions, a passage or verse at a time, as a way of encountering God and following that faint voice.

Pete and I didn't talk about God or religion. In retrospect, that's puzzling because he was deeply spiritual. Certainly no subject seemed unapproachable in the trusting and intimate relationship Pete and I developed. Perhaps my writing told him I was exploring this aspect of my life successfully, and he didn't want to intrude. Perhaps we perceived God differently and Pete hesitated to impose his personal beliefs into my journey. I'm not sure, but for whatever reason our conversations never moved in that direction.

So Pete and I hacked our way through the concerns and questions that haunted me and constantly threatened to return me to darkness. And he kept cycling back to that same nonsense question, listening patiently as I explained why I couldn't possibly contact Becky.

PETE

At the same time, my writing turned in an unanticipated direction. It was no longer just a tool with which to banish the demons, my words assumed a deeper purpose. I desired to listen more clearly to that voice whispering in the trees and make sense of my response. Finally I began to understand at heart-level what it meant to believe that God had been with me throughout this entire horrific experience. I needed to express the meaning and character of that voice and the journey on which it guided me.

IS THIS WHO I THINK IT IS?

I lived the center of the storm, and I still couldn't determine with certainty how it all came together. How did a journey from a place of complete chaos pass through so much pain and lead to the sort of peace that somehow settled around me? How could I possibly explain to someone else what made so little sense to me?

I did everything possible to sabotage my recovery, to drive away the people committed to helping me, to bury myself deeper in embarrassment, isolation, and sadness; instead I found myself surrounded by friends, contentment, and a life full of possibilities beyond my most unimaginable fantasies. I believed I was broken beyond repair; somehow I became whole again. I was convinced life had ended; now it seemed it was just beginning.

How would I ever communicate to her what this journey involved, where I traveled, and where I arrived?

CHAPTER 14

CENTER

This sort of writing provided a completely unfamiliar experience. Several past attempts to keep a journal fizzled for lack of sincerity. I think I knew for a long time that something was missing, but I had no idea what I was seeking or where to begin my search.

My life consisted of a hollow shell that appeared sound on the outside but lacked substance to fill the inner void. I became quite adept at maintaining the illusion, polishing the outer surface as though I could deceive myself into believing a pleasing exterior might replace interior emptiness.

My previous journaling followed a similar pattern of self-deception. Rather than honestly dismantling the walls that concealed inner despair, I wrote what I thought I was supposed to write. I attempted to sound thoughtful and profound, an odd approach since I would never have considered allowing anyone to read this half-hearted meandering. But even my private thoughts fell prey to my habit of focusing on appearance rather than substance.

Of course I wasn't fooling myself, and this dishonest exercise only enhanced the sense of powerlessness and reinforced the notion that something was wrong. I didn't write to discover answers; I simply augmented my efforts to look good while hiding from others and from myself. I ran from the light in my pursuit of shadows.

But as Pete and I broke down the barriers and exposed the emptiness, maintaining the outward appearance required too much effort. Pretending consumed so much energy for so long, and I couldn't maintain the facade any longer. I finally realized I didn't want to continue my participation in this self-defeating delusion.

I didn't reach a courageous, conscious decision based on some sudden influx of wisdom or insight. I didn't thoughtfully analyze my former approach and decide I ought to try a different strategy. I wouldn't have known how or where to begin that sort of life-altering transformation.

The change in attitude was truly an act of surrender. I simply gave up and accepted that whatever I evaded couldn't possibly be as fearsome as the emptiness and loneliness. I still had no idea what I was seeking, but the time to begin the search had arrived.

Surrender, giving up, giving in—whatever else it represented, in the end I made a choice based on faith. At first, I acted on a desperate belief that the agony of hiding was worse than whatever might happen if I stepped (or rolled) out of the shadows. Slowly, with nearly as many steps backward as forward, that conviction developed and matured until at last I understood that something greater than my anxiety guided me.

I didn't actively seek this assurance; I didn't design it and I certainly didn't expect it. This newfound faith was simply present, a gift of God's grace, ready to surround me with a fresh perspective as soon as I accepted its reality. I was sinking onto those church steps again, still lost and alone after all that had occurred over nearly two decades.

I confronted once more that prison door locked tight by my own fear, but I faced distinctly different circumstances. I was finally prepared to release the fear, to discover what it might mean to lean on God, and to walk by faith. I was prepared to explore what that faith might mean in the context of a damaged body and a broken spirit.

I know Jesus stood beside me every moment through heartbreak, injury, fear, and depression. He laughed with me, cried with me, and struggled with me. At every turn, He was ready to support me, love me, and show me how to use my get-out-of-jail-free card.

While I tried everything I could to hide the emptiness, God patiently offered to expose the void and fill it with peace and freedom. I did nearly everything wrong, but God's grace, His *Relentless Grace*, overwhelmed my mistakes and stubbornness.

This story would be incomplete without some discussion of the journal that developed from my counseling experience. For several months I could scarcely wait for the opportunity to read, ponder, digest, and then write about my personal thoughts and discoveries. Pete and I wrangled with the issues brought into focus by the accident, and during those endless therapy sessions I confronted and slowly vanquished self-created demons.

As my inner world calmed, I was free at last from the anguish and depression that crippled me more than any physical injury. The freedom and honest self-examination were unfamiliar, fresh, and energizing. As I tapped away at my keyboard, I experienced peace so foreign that I hadn't even been aware of its absence. In the midst of this peace, I was finally able to transfer my knowledge of God from head to heart. I wasn't just thinking about Him; for the first time I experienced an *encounter* with Him. That deeply personal encounter eventually healed me and set me free.

A friend recommended a book called *Journey to Center* by Thomas Crum. Crum described his attempt to live a "centered" life, asserting that from this place of center he could approach situations and decisions calmly and in concert with his principles and beliefs. He described his mental image of a place in which he could approach life from a centered perspective.

I found myself attracted to the idea of a centered life. As I considered what this concept might mean for me, I wrote these thoughts in my journal:

Any real movement toward center must involve seeking God, because God is the center. The primary objective of a centered life is a deeper relationship with God.

My journey is centered to the extent that it approaches God's design. From the perspective of a close relationship to God, I can better explore what it means to operate in harmony with my beliefs and deal with choices and circumstances in a manner consistent with my identity as a child of God.

"Center" represents something more than a New Age notion of self-actualization, an effort to become the best I can become. A search for center cannot focus on seeking myself, because "I" am not the center. A quest for self is doomed to be unsatisfying.

Real significance, the kind of significance that fills the soul, cannot be found within myself, because it's not there. A life centered on self cannot be truly meaningful, not because life lacks meaning, but because the meaning exists elsewhere.

I recalled the story of a boy who was looking for something under a streetlight. A man came along and offered to help. "Do you have any idea where you dropped it?" the man asked.

"Over there," said the kid, pointing to a dark area down the street.

So the man asked, "Why are you looking here?"

"Because," the kid replied, "the light is better here!"

Seeking CENTER within myself is like looking under the street-light for something that isn't there; it's an easier place to search, but I won't find what I'm seeking. Looking elsewhere might be more difficult, but at least I have the possibility of success.

If I really wish to find something, I have to seek in the proper location. If I really wish to find the CENTER, I have to seek where the center is located. I have to seek God.

I became intrigued by the notion of a physical location I might imagine when I wish to be more centered, closer to God, and what He wants for me. I began to consider my own mental vision of that centered place.

One day I was riding my hand cycle on a bike trail. I stopped for a drink, and as I looked around, I experienced a sense of peace and tranquility. I surveyed a location that could serve as the image for my place of center. Mentally recreating these calm, serene surroundings might help me to visualize and express in more concrete terms what it means to become closer to God and to what He intended for me. I began to analyze my experiences and write about my thoughts in terms of this place of center.

I imagined my mental "center" next to a path along a river. I could sit in the warm sunshine, or in the cool shade beneath a dense canopy of trees, solitary and isolated from the world around. Simply being in such placid surroundings prompted me to reflect, slow down, and become more aware.

The path disappeared into the woods. I could not see the approach from either direction. People appeared on the path, biking, skating, running, or walking. They traveled slowly or pushed their pace to extremes. Some seemed immersed in the beauty of this place; others focused on the path, their workout, or their destination. Some traveled alone, some in pairs or groups; they were friendly, or indifferent, or even rude.

I realized that the path and the people were not about me. They were not mine to control; it was not my job to figure out why they were here or whether they were traveling the proper route. I was free to greet each person without judgment, secure in the knowledge that God had created the path and the people on it.

The river assumed different forms. Sometimes it churned with anger and danger, sweeping away anything in its path. At other times it babbled pleasantly and invited me to listen and become absorbed in its kindness and peace. Sometimes it dwindled to a slow, dried-up trickle, barely alive among rocks and mud.

I realized that the river is what it is. I could fear the torrent, worry about being carried off, wonder about flooding and destruction here or anywhere. I could fret when the flow diminished, imagining drought and hunger, emptiness and despair, certain that it would never change. I could become mesmerized by the pleasant bubbling sounds on a lazy summer day and forget the danger and fear. None of this impacted the river.

> *Be still and know that I am God.*
>
> —Psalm 46:10

> *I am who I am.*
>
> —Exodus 3:14

I thought this changing state of the river had something important to teach me. I wrote some of my observations about the river:

> *The river is what it is and goes where it goes, as God is who He is and does what He does. Nothing I say or think or do changes it. God, like the river, just is.*

> *I am paralyzed with fear that I might be engulfed, as though the fear will somehow protect me or change the river's impact. I worry about its course after it passes, as though the worry will alter the river's direction.*

> *I lose hope when the flow diminishes, certain that there will never again be enough. I complain that it's not fair, that the same river destroys some and nourishes others with no seeming regard for merit.*

I cry to the heavens, as though on my advice God ought to change the nature and destination of the river He created. I'm certain that I know the very best state for the river. I question God's wisdom and purpose when the river flows in such obviously "wrong" ways.

The river originates beyond my understanding and travels beyond my understanding. It is infinite, created by an infinite God. I know that the river is what it is, and will go where it will go, and that it was created for and works for good.

The river just is, yet I struggle to accept it.

As I sit quietly in this place. I can gradually stop trying to change what I cannot change. As I allow myself to more fully BE in this place, I become more aware. I can watch and listen to the river in whatever state it exists, learning while asking nothing of it. I can trust that God, who created it, knows its proper path. Fear and worry diminish.

The river is what it is. I am detached from it, feeling no desire to alter it, aware that the river is not me, that I am not determined by its state or responsible for its course. The goals become awareness and acceptance rather than control and a self-centered need to know WHY.

I began to believe that this mental place of center could impact my perspective on nearly every important aspect of my life. I wondered about the character of the metaphor that made it speak so directly to my heart. I identified three aspects to this image, each representing a fundamental element of my identity.

I am fully functioning and "centered" when I am in relationship: with others, with myself, and with God. I am enriched to the extent that those relationships are open, honest, agenda-free encounters.

This is what I experience mentally in my place of center. Those traveling on the path represent the people that enter my life and my relationships with others. The place where I sit in solitude signifies my relationship with myself. The river concretely characterizes my relationship with infinite God.

This place by the river and the path speaks to my identity, who I AM as a creature created by God in his image. I am centered, whole and at peace when I am in relationship, because that is who I am and how I was created.

Being centered means being here, right now, with another, with myself, with God. When I remind myself to "sit by the river," I'm remembering to claim the identity inherent in my nature as a person created in the image of God who values relationship.

This notion of center dominated my thinking and writing for a considerable time. The image spoke about every facet of my existence. I became immersed in its implications and applications. I experienced a wonderful sense of peace as I envisioned myself in this mystical place of center.

The metaphor offered a structure that brought order to a previously chaotic jumble as I wandered through a lifetime of thoughts and feelings. This process of reading, analyzing, and writing had an amazing settling effect. I felt free to trust that this was exactly what I was supposed to be doing. I wasn't concerned with destination or outcome. I didn't consider how my ideas or activities might appear to others. I felt clearly that my exploration was guided by God's Spirit; that was sufficient.

Eventually, my exploration turned in another significant direction. I never "blamed" God for my injury, but the question was impossible to avoid: "Why did this happen?" An investigation appeared inevitable, and I began my journal entry with a connection to the image of center:

God does not decide every detail about who comes down the path, every decision they make, every move, every reaction. God doesn't determine whether a free throw is made, whether I guess right on my algebra test, or whether my numbers come up in the lottery.

God didn't decide that my injury should happen. He did not get up with me that Saturday and resolve that he would tear my life apart. He did not push me off that roof, bring up a gust of wind, cause me to slip, randomly decide to bring on a seizure, or do whatever caused my freak accident.

A god who operated like that would be a monster and could not possess the characteristics that are evident in God's historical revelation. Such a being is inconsistent with God as He has revealed Himself in my life. Why would I worship or seek relationship with such a capricious, arbitrary cosmic bully? How could the river that brings such peace be created and guided by that sort of tyrant?

I was a bit surprised by the certainty of my convictions. I could see that God had been preparing the groundwork and building a foundation of knowledge that would support me when I was finally ready to stand on it. I thought back to all of those Sundays following the night on the church steps, listening to Al teach about the character of this God who whispered to me in the breeze.

As I confronted this difficult question, I explored some of the sad misconceptions I'd encountered:

God is often portrayed as some sort of celestial gumball machine. You put your stuff in, crank the handle, and see what you get back. Then you bury yourself in wondering and worrying about why you got what you got and the other guy got what he got, trying to determine what to put into the machine the next time so you get what you want.

And since the machine's output so frequently doesn't match the input, at least from our short-term perspective, we waste considerable time and effort trying to make sense of nonsense based on our assumptions about fairness.

So what about my injury? How does infinite, omniscient, all-powerful God allow such an event? Why does the river nourish. some who don't deserve it while casting others upon its rocks, dashing them in seemingly random and unpredictable directions? Why does it dry up and allow good people to wither in the dust?

Why do bad things happen to good people?

Complex and difficult questions to be sure, but the basic answers seem relatively simple. Evil perverted the Creation. Without getting into the theology of original sin and the apple and the story of Adam and Eve, it's obvious that the Creation doesn't operate as God intended. Evil exists.

Call it what you want—Satan, the devil, hell, whatever. The enemy exists, and because it exists, the Creation is broken and doesn't conform to God's intentions. Events occur that were never part of the plan. Pain, suffering, broken relationships, disease—are all a result of evil that twists the Creation.

I recalled a conversation with a friend who visited me soon after I went home from the hospital, yet another piece of that foundation upon which I could draw as I arranged the pieces of this complex puzzle. I wrote about her comments to me:

When I fell on my head and shattered three vertebrae, evil won a temporary victory. God did not create me in His own image so I could experience that sort of pain. I simply do not believe that He intended for it to work this way. Everything I understand about God makes me absolutely certain that this injury was not His work.

Why does He allow it? I don't know. Mystery exists in the reaches of infinity. He is an infinite God. I'm not. It's His river. I'm OK with allowing the WHY to be God's responsibility. I'm only certain that He works within the Creation for good, and that in all circumstances He desires and works toward whole, healthy relationships.

And we know that in all things God works for the good of those who love him, who have been called according to his purpose.
                                        —Romans 8:27–29

God didn't cause my injury, just as He doesn't cause drunk driving accidents. But we can take hope from the knowledge that He won't waste our pain. He promises that we can trust Him to turn even the worst tragedy toward good.

As I worked through this difficult material, I recalled the times friends had tried to comfort me by voicing their belief that there was a reason for all of this, that my injury was a small part of the big picture of God's work in the world. I'm certain those folks meant well, but I had a different view:

I can't count the number of times someone tried to console me by explaining that my experience is part of God's plan. I'm supposed to take solace in the knowledge that God meant this to happen, that my injury needed to happen for God to advance His ultimate vision of the universe.

I'm especially amazed when I'm told that perhaps something good was meant to come from it because someone else will benefit or learn an important lesson through my pain. This logic is supposed to provide a coherent reason for my injury, and I guess that's supposed to make it easier to accept. In fact, I probably ought to celebrate and be thankful for my disability since it advanced God's work.

Baloney! There's no evidence that God capriciously selected me to be crippled so my students can better understand how to deal with disabled persons. No evidence that He did it to "teach me a lesson." No evidence that He ripped up the lives of those closest to me as a required portion of some cosmic curriculum.

There may be some limited form of comfort in believing that terrible events are part of "God's plan." But that sort of human-created consolation can't bring true peace or a closer relationship with God, because it denies the character of God as He's revealed Himself in Jesus Christ.

All I understand of God convinces me that He suffered when I fell. That's the point of Jesus. He understands the pain and fear. He struggled with me as I recovered. He walked, or "rolled," beside me as I returned to work and faced embarrassment and frustration. He carried me when I wanted to give up. He simply didn't mean for it to be this way.

As I operated in this peaceful, secure mental and emotional state, I experienced a powerful sense of Jesus' presence. I imagined that this was the same phenomenon I encountered in my hospital room when I awoke from my semi-coma and felt the reality of Jesus' love. I wasn't able then to lean on Him and claim the freedom that accompanied a personal relationship with Him.

But in the newly discovered inner stillness, I also found an awareness of Jesus that had been absent in my daily life. This awareness seemed to create a quiet confidence in stark contrast to the crashing uncertainty that previously overwhelmed me. As I rested in the security of this relationship, I wondered how Jesus would view my metaphor of center:

Jesus knew about center. When Satan tempted Him, the issues were the same: Why not shortcut the process, just this once; why shouldn't you make it turn out like you want? God can't really mean for you to feel this bad, can He? Why would He place all of the angels at your disposal if He didn't want you to call on them when you're tired or in pain?

Jesus knew the eternal nature of the river and the truth. As He moved through His adult ministry and became aware of His identity and destiny, He had every opportunity to alter the path, change the horrible outcome, and avoid the suffering He knew was coming. Why didn't He protect Himself from all that pain, especially since He didn't deserve any of it?

Jesus knew perfectly what I am only able to imagine with my limited mind. He knew that real peace and power lie in relationship with God, in valuing what God values, in making choices that are consistent with my nature as a creature of relationship. He experienced eternal, intimate fellowship with God from the beginning. He knew that there was no peace to be gained from any choice that diminished that relationship.

As a final thought on the subject, I wrote about the notion that my injury was somehow God's judgment of me for all of the mistakes I'd made, things I'd done that were wrong, sins great and small:

God is not about coercion. God wants me to be whole, happy, and free, and His revelation makes it clear how I can accomplish that. God is too often characterized as threatening; "Do what I command or else" comprises a common misperception of God's message. God doesn't threaten.

However, God does make it clear that His Creation has rules and actions have consequences. I tell a child not to touch the fire because he'll burn his hand. That's not a threat, it's education intended to help the child to avoid pain. God tells me certain actions will harm me because He loves me and wants the best for me. Sometimes the message seems so simple: Here's how I created you, here's what will ultimately make you happy and whole.

"But WHY?" I reply. "Why can't I just do as I wish?" That question is as silly as the child asking why he can't touch the fire if he wishes. Why does sin have consequences? Why didn't God make it different? Because you can't value relationship and just do as you please. Because the way you treat yourself, others, and God matters.

But God coerced and threatened Adam and Eve, didn't He? Nope. He tried to keep them safe from the evil He knew was present. He knew the harm that would come to them if they followed their own desires and reasoning. God's command to avoid the tree and its fruit wasn't a threat designed to control them. It was a warning to those He loved. God knew the consequences, the potential twisting of the good He intended, and He wanted them to avoid the pain.

God also doesn't "punish." Punishment is artificial, designed to coerce someone into following a certain path out of fear. "Don't touch the fire or I'll hit you" is a confusing message. Does that imply that it's OK to touch the fire as long as nobody else knows I did it?

"Hitting" is punishment, while the burn from the fire is a consequence. I don't think God ever "hits" me to frighten me into doing what He wants, but He does communicate clearly that my decisions and actions have worldly and eternal consequences.

Jesus didn't threaten or coerce people into accepting Him. He stayed with them, hung out, and allowed their experience to show them the truth. Their lives didn't change because of what He said, but because they felt the freedom of relationship with Him.

Looking back, those months assumed a mystical quality, something like a retreat experience that's impossible to maintain. I met God in my heart, and for a short time allowed His Spirit to guide and heal me. At some point, this magical time of retreat and self-examination faded a bit, and somehow that seemed right as well. I suspect I needed time to digest all that had happened.

After so many years of feeling lost, I finally felt at home. I still faced tough issues. The injury didn't magically disappear, and its effects continue to impact every facet of my life. Depression doesn't just go away, and I will deal forever with its potential to drag me back into the darkness. A lifetime of habitually hiding from myself had taken its toll, and I need to guard carefully against falling back into old patterns when circumstances threaten to overwhelm me. Life still wasn't a movie with a happily-ever-after ending.

But a page had been turned, and my life was different. Scrambling from one crisis to another was no longer my only option. I discovered a structure on which to base my choices and a meaning to fill the void in my soul. I'd still struggle, be tempted, and even fail. But somehow that was all right. I didn't need to be perfect anymore, and that realization made it easier to simply be me.

I was still seeing Pete. I'd given up wondering when the counseling would end and when I'd be "fixed." I was comfortable with the notion that this was another important part of the process and we would be done when we were done. My need to see some sort of linear progression from "broken" to "healed" slowly disappeared, replaced with a calm assurance that whatever was happening was just what was needed at the time. I seemed immersed in a sense of serenity.

The serenity, however, wasn't perfect. There was still that one nagging issue. That inscrutable psychologist's smile wasn't going to go away easily, and apparently one monster remained to be confronted.

IS THIS WHO I THINK IT IS?

As I wrote, a life that frequently had made no sense began to assume a direction that had been obscured by the noise of my story, my depression, and my injury. Pointlessness was supplanted by purpose, desperation by calm, panic by an unfamiliar confidence. Instead of simply surviving, I was thriving.

Who could have imagined that this horrible experience could lead to such peace? How did so circuitous a path through the darkness finally arrive at this incredible love?

Would any of this make any sense to her?

CHAPTER 15

THAT PESKY QUESTION

Pete and I wrestled with numerous difficult issues over several years. Divorce, my mom's death, depression, my injury, "Becky"—and no matter where our conversations and my writing wandered, we always seemed to circle back to that same pesky question: "Why don't you get in touch with her?"

For a long time, the question seemed silly and the answer remained static; no matter how much progress we made in other areas, this aspect of the conversation cycled around and around. But I noticed a subtle change.

As hope displaced depression, my often-rehearsed answer to Pete's question began to feel less certain. I still offered the same "logical" rationale for not intruding in her life, but the logic became less compelling. I started to wonder whether the question was really as dumb as I'd imagined. Gradually, another subtle change occurred, and the question became one I asked of myself. Why *didn't* I contact her?

Gradually I realized that I had no answer that made any sense. Not only had I failed to convince Pete, I now couldn't even convince myself.

I spent quite a bit of time thinking, writing, and talking about this development. I had no idea about her circumstances or where her path had taken her, and I wanted to be certain of my own motives and expectations. Eventually, though, I became quite clear about what needed to happen.

The Internet is amazing. With a small amount of information and a little persistence, one can find nearly anything or anyone. So I sat at my desk one day with an e-mail address and a choice. Should I really take this step into such unknown and potentially dangerous territory? How can I be certain it's the right thing to do?

I held that e-mail address for several weeks, then decided that there was no point to waiting any longer. So I typed a few sentences and, before I talked myself out of it, pressed *send* to launch my simple message into cyberspace.

It didn't take long. Within a couple of hours, a reply arrived. I took a deep breath. What kind of Pandora's Box had I opened?

I reached for the mouse, slowly selected the return message and clicked.

I stared at the words, the culmination of twenty years of searching, wondering, giving up, and hoping again: "Is this who I think it is?"

IS THIS WHO I THINK IT IS?

What in the world does she mean?

I couldn't sit and stare at the single line forever. No hidden meaning appeared between the simple words. I'd turned them over, around, and inside out, and I still didn't know precisely what her simple question meant.

If I was to make any more sense of the mystery of this message, I had to respond. This required a clever comeback:

Well, that depends. Who do you THINK it is?

What would she do with *that*?

EPILOGUE

The little mountain chapel was the sort of idyllic place you couldn't make up because no one would believe it. A simple high-pitched roof, a bell, and a small cross to identify it, blended so well with its surroundings that you easily passed on the road without noticing. Tucked away in the woods next to a mountain stream, just the right place to compose the last chapter in this portion of a most unlikely tale. I stole a moment to sit alone, away from our small group of friends and family.

The water splashing across the rocks below was pristine snow just hours ago. Two kayakers paddled easily with the calm, trouble-free current, but their skills would be challenged farther along. Maybe fifty yards upstream a fisherman stood in waders, flicking his line into a pool beneath some aspen trees.

The crushed-rock path from the road to this small clearing wasn't meant for a wheelchair, but these few moments alone, before the excitement of the day, justified the effort. This quiet forest made a fine spot to meditate and recall some of the significant trials and tests that marked the course leading to this improbable day.

I recalled that misty morning more than twenty-two years ago, peering through the fog, looking for the mountains that would mark entry into the Promised Land. I had no idea that I would sit here in the midst of those same mountains so many years later with the clanging fear of that icy morning replaced by perfect tranquility. We thought all those years ago that the mountains would be the place of a new life, but abandoned the dream in the face of two decades of separate corridors and blind alleys and doorways opened, shut, or slammed in our faces.

Two courses, as different as they could possibly be, leading from that morning to this charming little church. No way to project forward from either trail to this day. No way to get here from there, yet here we've arrived.

The unforeseen routes from those disparate pathways to this day commenced from unlikely origins—a pair of computer screens more than a thousand miles apart. Two frightened, lonely souls found a faint glimmer of hope in an almost-never-sent message, hope born in a long-ago dream and nurtured through months of e-mail messages. The communication was cautious at first, with no idea of the paths we'd each traveled, what old scars might be exposed and ripped open, or what new wounds might spring from this leap into uncharted territory. Gradually, the writing became more vulnerable as two people who once imagined sharing a new life now revealed the stuff of separate existences, the events and then the pains of twenty years frequently not truly lived but scarcely survived.

Hope first born in a vision cast aside but never quite forgotten. And slowly, as layers of carefully constructed defenses fell away, we discovered something incredible—hope blossomed, and in its flower we were astonished to find the dream. We peered through the mist again, expecting the Promised Land, finally ready for that new life together. And this time, neither asked, "Are we there yet?" fearful that if we didn't arrive soon the entire fantasy would disappear in the fog.

This time we knew where the mountains were. This time no fears or uncertainties chased us down the road, threatening to pounce if we stopped for even a moment. No frenzied, gotta-find-it-right-now-or-it'll-get-away searching. This time the dream could grow and mature, stand up to the past, and grow stronger as we learned about twenty years' worth of seeking, not-finding, losing, and seeking again, until we had both wearied of the process and believed we'd never find.

This time God comprised the basis of the dream. The night on the church steps, the handmade wooden cross, years of knowing that Jesus had walked with us; this history gave depth and substance to the dream, anchored it, and gave it a place to live. And because Jesus was now at its center, the dream could finally offer us a place to live.

The months of e-mail gave way to phone calls, and then to guarded meetings. With each step the fantasy became more real, until we could hold the vision only by holding each other. That improbable dream, almost but not quite lost, guided us from lives of hopelessness to this simple chapel in the midst of the mountains we sought so desperately but never quite reached. The dream matured during more than two years since *Is this who I think it is?*

A giggle from behind interrupted my reverie. Becky's nephew, bored already with waiting, brought his dad to throw stones into the river. There's something magical about dads and small boys splashing rocks in the water. I watched them for a moment, and then I had to leave, to finish preparing. I wore a polo shirt from home, but I'd need something a bit nicer even for our casual ceremony. I had worn a necktie maybe once or twice since the accident, since I couldn't tie the things anymore. My brother waited to help me, and then Becky and I would be ready to go forward together into this "impossible dream."

This was a day for remembering. I was delighted by my brother's presence, and I recalled another time I asked Jim for his help, one of the few coherent memories from the awful days in intensive care prior to my surgery. I was strapped into what's known as a Stryker bed, designed to rotate side to side to relieve pressure on a motionless body. I had no control of my arms, and my head was attached to weights keeping traction on my neck to protect it from further injury.

And of all things, *my ear itched*! I couldn't scratch it, and it was driving me nuts. Jim came into the room and I asked him to scratch my ear for me. He told me they'd specifically been told not to touch me because of the danger of further injury.

"C'mon, my ear itches. Just scratch my ear."

"Nope, can't do it."

I demanded, "Scratch my ear!"

"Please don't keep asking. I can't, they told us not to touch you."

Interesting that I'd recall such an insignificant event out of the myriad important episodes of this chronicle-turned-fairy tale. Well, today my brother could touch my ear if he wanted as he helped me get dressed for this magical celebration.

He told me he was practicing a nice double knot for my necktie. I appreciated his help with shoelaces and shirt buttons, and things that weren't yet part of the long list of tasks I'd learned to accomplish with my altered body. Then he would light a candle on the altar to remember our mom and stand beside me as I rolled into the New World. I valued his love and support, and now I could scratch my own ear when it itched!

Inside, the sanctuary was simple and basic. There was old creaky wood everywhere. Our guests filled seven rows of carved pews facing a simple wooden altar. Flute and piano music played by two former students which filled the room beneath the high, wood-slat ceiling. Another connection in the web of people that made this day possible—the flute player was Megan's brother, Aaron, my second "coffee kid." I watched from the back as people signed the guest book, greeting a few, but mostly just taking it all in. I heard giggling as Becky and her sisters got ready in the next room.

Tom climbed down the stairs from the small loft where he created a makeshift sound system for some special music. He flashed that same goofy grin that once made me wonder what kind of hippie had appeared at my door. The hair was a lot shorter and his old VW bus had been replaced by another classic, a 1972 Buick convertible. That silly smile increased the joy of this amazing day.

Pete entered, sporting one of his trademark Hawaiian shirts. On this day there was no doubt about the meaning of the broad smile. We exchanged a few quiet words and a big hug. I could see genuine pleasure as he shared this commemoration of a new beginning. He wouldn't hang around for the party because he carefully separated personal and professional issues, but I was thrilled that he joined our celebration.

As Becky and I designed this day, we envisioned being surrounded by a circle of family and friends. To compile our guest list, we asked each other who needed to be present to complete the circle. This day might never have materialized without Pete's help. His presence in our circle was essential.

Is This Who I Think It Is?

Thanks in large measure to Pete's wisdom and quiet guidance, we now knew the answer to that question.

I thought back to the church steps and Hank's decision to alter his plans that evening. I never talked to him after our conversation, and I wondered whether he had any idea of the difference he made. He wasn't in our circle, but this gathering would not have been possible without his kindness on that desperate night. I marveled that one person and one chance meeting could so powerfully impact the direction of an entire lifetime.

Of course, I don't really believe that "chance" had much to do with that encounter. God brought me to those steps, just as he brought Becky and me to this day of joy and celebration.

Al placed his hand on my shoulder. Getting him back to Colorado from his church in California required a bit of scrambling and rescheduling, but he had to be there. This circle couldn't be complete in his absence. He had to be the pastor to escort us across the threshold and into our new life.

We smiled together. Al and I shared a difficult journey. We traveled from the early days as he helped me understand a personal God and through those terrible days in the hospital. We enjoyed a gentle friendship born of shared struggle, shared faith, and the quiet contentment of two lives finally at rest.

No more "monster in the mirror." Al assured me so long ago that "I" was in there somewhere; that "I" wasn't the Frankenstein screws and the half-alive skeleton that stared back at me. He was right, though neither of us could have possibly known how long I'd search before I found "me" in the midst of a broken life.

More than anyone else, Al appreciated the significance of this occasion. This improbable episode symbolized much more than two people who worked their way through difficult times and managed to find happiness at the edge of darkness. Our gathering represented more than the fulfillment of an old dream, more than love and commitment shared by two souls too long apart.

Our celebration was about God's work in two lives, about promises made and kept that we would never walk (or roll) alone, and that hope flowers even in the most desperate of times. Not just wishing for something better, but real hope, the kind of expectation that can carry us through the pain of evil and the damage brought about by our own unfortunate choices.

This day was about claiming those promises, about committing in return to lean at least a bit more on the true source of authentic hope. God's precious gift of unmerited hope guided us on a path we could never have discovered by ourselves, from that morning in the fog to this glorious, cloudless afternoon.

This improbable day was about God's *Relentless Grace*.

"Ready?" Al asked.

"Absolutely." This moment was more than twenty years in the making. Twenty years of dreams and disappointments. Twenty years of wishing and giving up and no-hope. Twenty years since that frantic question: "*Where are the mountains?*"

EPILOGUE

Finally, we found them. We were home.
Thank God.

> *Forget the former things; do not dwell on the past. See, I am doing
> a new thing! Now it springs up; do you not perceive it? I am mak-
> ing a way in the desert, and streams in the wasteland.*
> —Isaiah 43:18–19

The Master's Hand

'Twas battered and scarred, and the auctioneer
Thought it scarcely worth his while
To spend much time with the old violin
But he held it up with a smile.

"How much am I bid, good folks?" he cried,
"Who'll start the bidding for me?
A dollar? A dollar! Now who'll make it two?
Two dollars! Now who'll make it three?

"Three dollars once, three dollars twice,
Going for three?" But no!
From the back of the room a gray haired man
Came forward and picked up the bow.

Then wiping the dust from the old violin,
And tightening the worn old strings,
He played a tune as sweet and pure
As a caroling angel sings.

The music ceased, and the auctioneer
In a voice that was quiet and low, said,
"Now what am I bid for the old violin?"
And he held it up with the bow.

"A thousand dollars? Now who'll make it two?
Two thousand! Now who'll make it three?
Three thousand once, three thousand twice,
Going, and gone," said he.

The people cheered, and some of them cried,
"We really do not understand.
What changed its worth?" Swift came the reply,
"The touch of a master's hand."

EPILOGUE

"There's many a man, with his life out of tune,
Battered and scarred by sin.
He's auctioned cheap to the thoughtless crowd,
Much like the old violin.

"A look, a touch, a glass of wine,
A game, and they travel on.
They're going once, they're going twice,
They're going, and almost gone.

"Then the master comes, and the foolish crowd
Never can quite understand,
The worth of a soul, and the change that is wrought
By the touch of The Master's hand."

—Myra Brooks Welch

To order additional copies of this title call:
1-877-421-READ (7323)
or please visit our Web site at
www.winepressbooks.com

If you enjoyed this quality custom-published book,
drop by our Web site for more books and information.

www.winepressgroup.com
"Your partner in custom publishing."